W9-CBM-916

The Beginner's Guide to Spiritual Warfare

The Beginner's Guide to Spiritual Warfare

- USING YOUR SPIRITUAL WEAPONS
- DEFENDING YOUR FAMILY
- RECOGNIZING SATAN'S LIES

NEIL T. ANDERSON and
TIMOTHY M. WARNER

Regal

From Gospel Light
Ventura, California, U.S.A.

PUBLISHED BY REGAL BOOKS
FROM GOSPEL LIGHT
VENTURA, CALIFORNIA, U.S.A.
PRINTED IN THE U.S.A.

Regal

Regal Books is a ministry of Gospel Light, a Christian publisher dedicated to serving the local church. We believe God's vision for Gospel Light is to provide church leaders with biblical, user-friendly materials that will help them evangelize, disciple and minister to children, youth and families.

It is our prayer that this Regal book will help you discover biblical truth for your own life and help you meet the needs of others. May God richly bless you.

For a free catalog of resources from Regal Books/Gospel Light, please call your Christian supplier or contact us at 1-800-4-GOSPEL *or* www.regalbooks.com.

Originally published by Servant Publications in 2000.

All Scripture quotations, unless otherwise indicated, are taken from the *Holy Bible, New International Version*®. Copyright © 1973, 1978, 1984 by International Bible Society. Used by permission of Zondervan Publishing House. All rights reserved.

Other versions used are
KJV—King James Version. Authorized King James Version.
LB—Scripture quotations marked (*LB*) are taken from *The Living Bible*, copyright © 1971. Used by permission of Tyndale House Publishers, Inc., Wheaton, IL 60189. All rights reserved.
NASB—Scripture taken from the *New American Standard Bible*, © 1960, 1962, 1963, 1968, 1971, 1972, 1973, 1975, 1977 by The Lockman Foundation. Used by permission.
NKJV—Scripture taken from the *New King James Version*. Copyright © 1979, 1980, 1982 by Thomas Nelson, Inc. Used by permission. All rights reserved.
NRSV—The Scripture quotations contained herein are from the *New Revised Standard Version Bible*, copyright 1989, by the Division of Christian Education of the National Council of the Churches of Christ in the U.S.A. Used by permission. All rights reserved.
Phillips—The New Testament in Modern English, Revised Edition, J. B. Phillips, Translator. © J. B. Phillips 1958, 1960, 1972. Used by permission of Macmillan Publishing Co., Inc., 866 Third Avenue, New York, NY 10022.

© 2000 Neil T. Anderson and Timothy M. Warner
All rights reserved.

Cover design by Alan Furst, Minneapolis, Minnesota

Library of Congress Cataloging-in-Publication Data
Anderson, Neil T., 1942–
  The beginners guide to spiritual warfare / Neil T. Anderson and Timothy M. Warner.
    p. cm.
  ISBN 0-8307-3387-6
  1. Spiritual warfare. I. Warner, Timothy M. II. Title.
  BV4509.5.A522 2004
  235'.4—dc22   2003027880

  2 3 4 5 6 7 8 9 10 11 12 13 14 15 / 09 08 07 06 05 04

Rights for publishing this book in other languages are contracted by Gospel Light Worldwide, the international nonprofit ministry of Gospel Light. Gospel Light Worldwide also provides publishing and technical assistance to international publishers dedicated to producing Sunday School and Vacation Bible School curricula and books in the languages of the world. For additional information, visit www.gospellightworldwide.org; write to Gospel Light Worldwide, P.O. Box 3875, Ventura, CA 93006; or send an e-mail to info@gospellightworldwide.org.

Contents

Introduction

We have just begun the third millennium, and most of the world has still not heard the Good News that Jesus came to set the captives free. Approximately one-third of this planet's sovereign nations are in serious conflict, and the numbers are rising. The church around the world is suffering greatly. More Christians were martyred for their faith in each of the last two years of the second millennium than in any other year of church history.

In America we are losing the drug war, and racial tensions continue to exist. Interpersonal tensions have erupted in unprecedented shootings in workplaces and on high school campuses. Marriages are failing and families are disintegrating. While doing research for two recent books, I discovered that we are experiencing a blues epidemic in an age of anxiety, and the problem is global. Even our churches have their struggles. Four hundred pastors in the United States are forced to resign every month. There are many casualties in the spiritual battle for the souls of God's people.

On the other hand, there are also many victories. We may be on the verge of the greatest revival this world has ever seen. Not since Pentecost have we seen such phenomenal worldwide church growth. Africa was less than 5 percent Christian at the beginning of the twentieth century. It is now, at the end of the second millennium, nearly 50 percent Christian. There were only about 5 million believers in China when the Communist regime took over. Now the estimates vary from 100 to as high as 150 million believers. Missiologists estimate that between 25,000 and 35,000 are coming to Christ daily in China. Indonesia is the world's most populated Muslim nation, but the percentage of Christians there has been increasing so rapidly that the government won't release accurate figures.[1]

The prayer movement that is sweeping this country may be one of the greatest signs of a coming revival. A great contribution to this prayer movement are the "Prayer Summits" begun by Joe Aldrich for pastors. Who would have thought even ten years ago that we could get pastors from different denominations to pray together for four days with no other agenda than to meet with God? Joe describes this phenomenon in his book *Prayer Summits.*[2]

Bill Bright, the founder and president of Campus Crusade for Christ, sensed God's leading to fast and pray for forty days. He was so moved by God during this time that he called many Christian leaders around the country to join him for three days of prayer and fasting. He was hoping that three hundred would come, but instead six hundred Christian leaders met in Orlando, Florida, on December 5-7, 1994. They represented more than one hundred different denominations and religious organizations. In his book, *The Coming Revival*, Bill shares the story and gives a clarion call for prayer and fasting. To prepare for the coming revival, he envisions five million people praying and fasting for forty days. Encouraged by the glowing testimonies he heard after the first prayer and fasting gathering, he called for another one in Los Angeles—this time 2,500 showed up. The next year 3,500 came to St. Louis, and this movement of prayer and fasting has been growing ever since.

Meanwhile, more than 2,500 Christian radio and television stations broadcast the gospel daily to an audience of 4.6 billion. I had the privilege of speaking to the staff of HCJB in Quito, Ecuador, at their annual meeting. I was impressed with their commitment and their technological expertise. The same holds for TransWorld Radio and Far Eastern Broadcasting, who are working together with HCJB to blanket this planet with the Good News. They can now package a radio station in a suitcase and broadcast the gospel anywhere in the world. We are the first generation that can say without reservation, "We have the technology to actually fulfill the Great Commission in our generation."

The Christian Broadcasting Network (CBN) has expanded overseas. CBN's founder, Pat Robertson, said it took twenty years to see a million people pray to receive Christ as a result of the network's ministry, but they have seen that number increase fifty times in five years (between 1990 and 1995). Billy Graham held a crusade via satellite that may have been heard by as many as 2.5 billion people. We have only scratched the surface of what can and most certainly will be done with satellite communication and the Internet.

Cooperation in ministry is another significant sign that we are in for a great harvest. We may be driving different cars, but we are all driving them in the same kingdom and getting our gas from the same station. There is a growing majority in the body of Christ who are sick and tired of Christians competing with or defeating one another. It is beyond the time for the church to personally appropriate the truth of Ephesians 4:1-6:

As a prisoner for the Lord, then, I urge you to live a life worthy of the calling you have received. Be completely humble and gentle; be patient, bearing with one another in love. Make every effort to keep the unity of the Spirit through the bond of peace. There is one body and one Spirit—just as you were called to one hope when you were called—one Lord, one faith, one baptism; one God and Father of all, who is over all and through all and in all.

God is preparing his people and pulling his church together for the final harvest. In the high priestly prayer, Jesus is praying that we will all be one just as he and the Father are one (see Jn 17:21). He is not praying for the old ecumenism which was diluted by liberalism. He is praying that the true born-again, Bible-believing community known as the body of Christ will work together to stem the tide of liberalism and immorality, the rising threat of the New Age, and the secular movement of universalism.

Caution must be taken not to water down the movement. Unity in the Spirit is not universalism. Paul says, "Do not be bound together with unbelievers; for what partnership have righteousness and lawlessness, or what fellowship has light with darkness? Or what harmony has Christ with Belial, or what has a believer in common with an unbeliever?" (2 Cor 6:14-15, NASB). We must maintain an unshakeable commitment to the authority of Scripture, and never compromise our character in order to produce results.

Mission America has the goal of praying for and sharing Christ with every person in our nation. That will be impossible unless the Holy Spirit draws the church together as partners in ministry. More than eighty denominations and two hundred parachurch ministries are cooperating to accomplish this task. This united effort to reach our nation for Christ is being called "Celebrate Jesus." We don't have to throw away our denominational distinctives or doctrinal beliefs to preserve the unity of the Spirit. But we do have to believe in "a renewal in which there is no distinction between Greek and Jew, circumcised and uncircumcised, barbarian, Scythian, slave and freeman, but Christ is all, and in all" (Col 3:11, NASB).

The only legitimate basis for unity within the body of Christ is the realization that every born-again Christian is a child of God. Cooperation will require forgiveness and reconciliation. It will necessitate toleration of other people's perspectives without compromising personal convictions. We must respect the denominational distinctives of others and relate with integrity in all matters.

Recently, I was conducting a conference for 1,500 pastors and missionaries in Bacalod, Philippines. A group of Filipino teenagers committed themselves to praying around the clock for the duration of the conference. They were on their knees pleading that their leaders upstairs would repent and agree to work together. I was never so humbled in my life! This should be the prayer of Christian leaders. Legitimate Christian leaders should desire unity in the body of Christ, which is the prayer of our Lord. Could it be that our Christian leadership may be the major stumbling block to world revival? Can the church rise above its leaders?

If you were the enemy, how would you work to defeat the church in its efforts to reach this world for Christ? Since the Bible teaches that a house divided against itself cannot stand (see Mk 3:25), the enemy will certainly work to divide us. First, he will work on our minds, since a double-minded man is unstable in all his ways (see Jas 1:8). Paul writes, "The Spirit clearly says that in later times some will abandon the faith and follow deceiving spirits and things taught by demons" (1 Tm 4:1). Then the enemy will seek to divide our marriages and our ministries. Is that happening?

Another sign of a great awakening is the growing awareness that "Our struggle is not against flesh and blood, but against the rulers, against the powers, against the world forces of this darkness, against the spiritual forces of wickedness in the heavenly places" (Eph 6:12, NASB). We may disagree about how to engage the enemy, but at least we are starting to agree that we all have one. Without this realization we are like blindfolded warriors striking out at each other and ourselves. We must never let the devil set the agenda, but we dare not underestimate his influence or allow the attitude, "the devil made me do it." We are responsible for our own attitudes and actions. Satan is a defeated foe, but he is also the god of this world, and "the whole world lies in the power of the evil one" (1 Jn 5:19, NASB). How are we going to reach this world for Christ if Satan has blinded the minds of the unbelieving (see 2 Cor 4:4)?

With all the moral corruption in the world, it is tempting to ask, "Why doesn't the Lord just come back and end all this?" I heard a retired African-American pastor give the correct answer to this question as he addressed a group of inner-city pastors after the Los Angeles riots that were prompted by the verdict of the Rodney King trial. As my memory serves me, he said, "Fifty years ago the Lord looked into the kingdom of darkness and he saw me. Had he come at that time, I would have been locked out of the kingdom of God for all eternity. The Lord is not slow about his promises. For him one day is as a thousand years. He is waiting for the gospel to go out to the ends of the earth, and then the end will come." We longingly look for the Lord's return, but how many of us still have a family member, a friend, a neighbor, or a coworker who doesn't know the Lord? How selfish it is for us to pray for his return before doing what we can in this life to see that all may hear the Good News.

Another tempting question is, "Why doesn't God do something?" What more does God need to do for the church to come alive in Christ and fulfill our purpose for being here? He has defeated the devil, sent Christ to die for our sins, given us eternal life, equipped us with the Holy Spirit, and provided the Manufacturer's Operating Manual (the Bible) which explains all the hows and whys. The missing ingredient is our response in repentance and faith. So, what are we waiting for? A new word from God? The canon of Scripture is closed! The next new word will probably come face-to-face. Power from on high? It already came, at Pentecost. Paul wrote, "I pray that the eyes of your heart may be enlightened, so that you know what is the hope of his calling, what are the riches of the glory of his inheritance in the saints, and what is the surpassing greatness of his power toward us who believe. These are in accordance with the working of the strength of his might" (Eph 1:18-19, NASB). We already have all the power we need to be and do all that he wants us to be and do. So let's "be strong in the Lord and in the strength of his might" (Eph 6:10, NASB).

Every day we face three enemies which threaten our faith in God: the world, the flesh, and the devil. In this book we will focus primarily on the work of Satan and the victory we have in Christ. The testimonies come from our experience in ministry, but the details have been changed to protect the identities of those involved. It is our prayer that you come to understand the nature of spiritual warfare in such a way that you will have confidence in God that the battle has already been won, and you will know how to stand firm in your faith.

Dr. Neil T. Anderson

ONE

A Reluctant Warrior?

So you are a beginner at this business of spiritual warfare. Join the club! We are all learners, to say the least, and we have all had to come through the process of learning to fight in this battle.

I (Tim) grew up in a family of eight children—four boys and four girls. I was the youngest of the boys. As a boy I was not a fighter. Not that there weren't opportunities. There were other boys in our neighborhood who were itching for a good fight. Once in a while I would throw some green apples at them, but usually I would run rather than fight.

When I finished high school, however, the United States was involved in the Second World War, and within ninety days of graduation I found myself in an army camp, learning to fight. I didn't mind the rigorous physical conditioning, but I hated the fighting part of army basic training. Targets on the rifle range at first were the usual circular ones with a bull's-eye in the middle. They soon became images of men, however, and I recoiled at the thought of shooting at another human being.

Then there was hand-to-hand combat, which we were to practice with our "combat buddy." It was with great reluctance that I tried to learn how to harm and even kill another man with my own hands.

What I hated most, though, was bayonet drill. I was taught to lunge at a straw-filled dummy, piercing it with the bayonet fixed on the end of my M-1 rifle, all the while snarling and growling like a ferocious animal. I could think of few things more repulsive than that. Yes, I was a reluctant warrior.[1]

A Reluctant Spiritual Warrior

Perhaps it was not surprising, then, that I carried that same attitude over into my spiritual life. I grew up in a thoroughly evangelical home and church, but I was taught not to be a fighter spiritually. The safe course was to stay "small and pure." When it came to things like Satan and demons, the safe course was to ignore them. It was easy to go overboard with such things, I was told, but this would not happen if I did not even talk about them.

Following my army experience, I entered a good evangelical college and majored in religious studies. This was followed by three years at a theological seminary that specialized in inductive Bible study. Two years after graduation from seminary I found myself on a freighter, sailing for missionary service in a tribal village in West Africa. I would soon find that nothing in my Christian upbringing, none of my biblical and theological study, and none of my professors had prepared me to function knowledgeably and effectively in the war I was entering. To be more accurate, I was not entering the war for the first time by becoming a missionary. I was only going to a place where the elements of battle were going to be much more overt and more difficult to handle. This was also a place where Satan's control over the people had not been seriously challenged. And I was still a reluctant warrior.

In fact, though I did not yet realize it, I was entering a situation not too much different from the combat zone of World War II. It was just that the armies were spiritual rather than physical. As a former soldier in the Allied army, I knew the sound of rifle and machine-gun fire. I knew the sound of incoming artillery shells. I had seen the dead and wounded bodies of my comrades. The spiritual dimensions and the casualties of the battle I was now entering would not be as obvious, but would be just as real and deadly. Unfortunately, I did not gain this perspective on missionary service until years later when studying spiritual warfare.

Oh yes, I knew Ephesians 6:12, which clearly told me that the real struggle was "not against flesh and blood, but against the rulers, against the authorities, against the powers of this dark world and against the spiritual forces of evil in the heavenly realms." And I not only knew it; I believed it. At least I would have given the correct answer to any question posed to me on that subject, but that truth had not yet moved from formal belief to functional belief.

My thirty-five years of involvement in Christian higher education have taught me that a person can successfully complete both Bible college and theological seminary and still have most of one's knowledge filed away in the filing cabinet of the brain, not operating in the control center of the heart. We all talk a better theology than we live out in daily life. Only the Lord himself had perfect integrity between profession and practice. In some cases, however, the chasm between profession and practice among us humans has become very wide and very deep.

Further complicating this problem is the fact that often we have not learned some key truth related to the Christian life, or we have had the truth twisted in some way by well-meaning but faulty teachers. In my own case, as a young believer I had had some problems in both areas. I certainly had not been led into a correct understanding of either my identity "in Christ" or my relationship as a believer to Satan and demons.

How Do You Keep Your Balance?

This weakness in the discipline of new believers reflects what I believe to be one of Satan's favorite tactics—namely, to cause us to view good and evil as opposite ends of a spectrum. The truth is that Satan creates evil by perverting what God created to be good, and he does this by pushing the truth to extremes in either of two opposite directions. This can be demonstrated on almost any subject one cares to explore, but on the subject of demons it comes down to the idea that demons are either behind everything or behind nothing. This is an attractive position, because the answers are always easier at the extremes. If demons are not functional parts of our world, then we don't have to even think about them. If they are behind all of our problems, then we simply need to learn to get rid of them. But if the truth is somewhere between those extremes, we need discernment to know what is demonic and what is the result of living in a fallen world. Such discernment involves a great deal more knowledge and carries much more responsibility than do the easy answers at the extremes.

Simon Peter's Wise Advice

Peter gives us some help with this in his first letter. As Peter writes, it is evident that he is an older and wiser man than the one we see during his experiences with Jesus in the Gospels. He has learned many things during his eventful life, and in this letter he is sharing some of that learning with his readers. After reviewing some basics of the gospel message, he gives a basic command: "Prepare your minds for action; be self-controlled" (1 Pt 1:13). This doesn't sound like the impulsive young man we encountered in the Gospels. No, he is indeed older and wiser. He has learned that the spiritual battle is a battle for the mind. Therefore, "Prepare your minds for action; be self-controlled."

At the end of the letter, he comes back to that same theme when he writes, "Be self-controlled and alert. Your enemy the devil prowls around like a roaring lion looking for someone to devour. Resist him, standing firm in the faith, because you know that your brothers throughout the world are undergoing the same kind of sufferings" (1 Pt 5:8-9). I am not sure how *resist* got changed to *ignore* in the thinking of so many believers. Certainly, if Satan could not do anything to "good Christians," as many have taught, Peter would have said something like, "Yes, we have this enemy, but don't worry about him. He can't do anything to you if you are a real believer."

I assume that Peter chose his words carefully, under the guidance of the Holy Spirit, and he commands us to be "self-controlled and alert" in relation to this enemy. *Self-controlled* is the same word he used in 1:13, and he uses it again in 4:7 in relation to being ready for "the end of all things." It is not insignificant that Paul says concerning the second coming of Christ that we should "be alert and self-controlled" (1 Thes 5:6). These are exactly the same words Peter uses here in speaking of our relation to the devil. His point is that while we do not know the time of the second coming, we should not be taken completely by surprise by it. We should be prepared to meet the Lord with no advance notice, whether that be in a secret rapture of the church or through a sudden death. I have been in several life-threatening automobile accidents. In none of them would I have had even ten seconds to make my peace with God. I needed to be up-to-date in my relationship with him so that I was ready to meet him at any moment, with no advance warning. I needed to be self-controlled and alert in view of the possibility that I could be called on to stand before the Lord with no time for special preparation.

Peter now tells us that we need to have the same attitude toward the devil, who is the "ruler" of this world. Peter is saying that we need to be *self-controlled and alert* because "the whole world lies in the power of the evil one" (1 Jn 5:19, NASB).

I think Martin Luther had the right perspective when he wrote in his famous hymn, "And though this world with devils filled should threaten to undo us, we will not fear, for God has willed his truth to triumph through us." To be alert to the activity of the enemy is not to be demon-centered. We are to be Christ-centered and stand firm in our faith. Our lives, like Luther's, are to be characterized by the confidence that in Christ we are more than conquerors (see Rom 8:37). This does not mean, however, that we can ignore a desperate enemy who is committed to the destruction of our witness and ministry.

Peter knew something about the enemy's tactics from his early experience as a disciple. You will remember that it was Peter to whom Jesus was relating when he said, "Get behind me, Satan!" (Mt 16:23). The clear implication is that Satan had been putting thoughts into Peter's mind without Peter realizing it. Jesus was alert to the way Satan operates and recognized the source of the thoughts. Peter obviously didn't. He had not yet learned to be self-controlled and alert. (In any case, it would be something of a shock to have Jesus say those words to you, wouldn't it?)

Peter may also have been reflecting on his experience of denying Christ at the time of his trial. In the Upper Room Peter had made the strongest assertions of his commitment to Jesus. "Even if all fall away on account of you, I never will," he said. And when Jesus predicted that Peter would actually deny him, Peter confidently affirmed, "Even if I have to die with you, I will never disown you" (Mt 26:35). Yet his pride caused him not to be self-controlled and alert a short time later when he was confronted about his relationship to Jesus by a couple of servant girls and others who were observing the trial. He not only denied that he was a follower of Jesus, he "began to call down curses on himself and he swore to them, 'I don't know the man!'" (Mt 26:74). He did not resist the tempter as he now commands us to do. Jesus suddenly was not Lord; he was just "the man." From his older-and-wiser perspective, Peter now speaks words of wisdom to all of us: "Be self-controlled and alert because you have an enemy that is out to destroy you."

Be Prepared to Fight

It is dangerous to be in a war zone if you are not prepared to meet the enemy. During the Second World War, I served with a unit that was "mopping up" pockets of enemy resistance that still existed after the main lines of battle had moved on. We would drive until we met such resistance, do whatever was needed to overcome it, and then move on. Because we never knew how far we would go before meeting the enemy, we had to be constantly on the alert for signs of enemy troops.

At one point in that process, our convoy of vehicles stopped. I was fairly far back in the long line of vehicles, so it was not possible to know what was happening at the front of the line. While we were stopped, a driver a few vehicles ahead of mine went to sleep, and when he woke up with a start, he discovered that the convoy had moved on without him. In his haste to catch up, he missed a turn and led the rest of us right into enemy-held territory. The problem was that we were not prepared to meet the enemy. The chaplain and I were traveling with the medics attached to the Service Company, with all kinds of supplies and equipment to support the combat troops, but we were not armed for battle. As a result, we had to turn around and beat a hasty retreat. That was not only embarrassing, it was dangerous.

Many Christians approach the spiritual enemy like this, however, and then they wonder why such bad things happen to them. It is bad enough to meet the enemy when you are prepared. It is quite another thing to meet him when you are *not* prepared. The problem is complicated when one is talking about spiritual warfare, because the enemy is not visible to the eyes. One normally doesn't have any problem identifying an enemy soldier or tank, although camouflage can be a bit tricky even with a physical enemy. With a spiritual enemy, however, the need for self-control and alertness increases significantly.

I learned something about this some years ago when I was in Reno, Nevada, for ministry in a church there. I was with several other men, and we decided to visit one of the famous gambling casinos—not to gamble, just to look, to be tourists. It was my very first exposure to such a place, and I was soon absorbed in all of the fascinating things going on around me. The dealers obviously were very skilled in handling the cards. The roulette wheels were more intriguing than the pictures I had seen of such things. One particular lady was playing three slot machines at the same time! She had a handful of coins in one hand, and she operated the lever on the machine with the other. She had obviously done this many times before, because she could put the coins in the slots and pull the levers in almost perfect rhythm. It was fascinating to watch her.

About this time, however, I began to ask myself, "What is going on here? Why are these people here? What are they looking for? What are they finding?" Suddenly my fascination with a tourist attraction turned to revulsion on the one hand and concern for the gamblers on the other. Part of me wanted to get out of that den of iniquity, and part of me wanted to rescue the people trapped in the snare of the enemy. I began to understand what Paul meant when he wrote to the Corinthians, "Christ's love compels us ... so from now on we regard no one from a worldly point of view" (2 Cor 5:14,16).

It is so easy to see only the human, physical side of life that we tend to forget that "what is seen is temporary, but what is unseen is eternal" (2 Cor 4:18). One of Satan's strategies is to get us to think and live within the limits of the time-space world. He has obviously been very successful with that strategy in the Western world. Our culture conditions us to think this way. Our public education is built on the premise that this is an evolved world, with no eternal perspectives, and religious matters therefore can be left out of the educational program without losing anything in the process.

That kind of thinking makes it easy to believe that we should ignore the devil instead of resisting him. The so-called Enlightenment thinking is not really enlightened at all. It is largely responsible for eliminating God and eternal truth from their central place. Paul warned, "See to it that no one takes you captive through hollow and deceptive philosophy, which depends on human tradition and the basic principles of this world rather than on Christ" (Col 2:8). There can be no doubt, however, that Peter's command is still valid, even in this "enlightened" age. We need to be self-controlled and alert when it comes to all things spiritual, and that includes our spiritual enemy the devil.

It's a World War

Another observation about this passage from Peter is that this battle is not limited to a few places in the world. Peter says that our "brothers throughout the world are undergoing the same kind of sufferings" at the hands of this enemy (1 Pt 5:9). Satan and demons are active not only in preliterate, tribal societies, but also in the sophisticated, enlightened Western world. Satan's tactics may change slightly in the West, but he is still committed to destroying the work of God any place and any time he finds an opportunity. Jesus said that this enemy comes to steal, kill, and destroy (see Jn 10:10), and he does not limit that activity to any geographic location.

So, while we do not see life dominated by Satan and his host of demons, neither do we assume that we can just ignore them. The biblical warnings about Satan and demons are all addressed to believers, and our basic attitude is to be one of self-control and alertness. To put it another way, we need to have spiritual discernment. We need spiritual eyesight to perceive when we are dealing with this crafty enemy.

Learning to Spot the Enemy

At this point someone may raise the objection, "Yes, but don't you have to have a lot of theological education to be able to do that? It is fine for you to say these things, but how can an 'ordinary Christian' expect to have that kind of discernment?"

Jesus had a rather simple answer to this question. He said that his sheep know the Shepherd's voice, "but they will never follow a stranger; in fact, they will run away from him because they do not recognize a stranger's voice" (Jn 10:4-5). Knowing the Shepherd's voice is not a matter of formal education. It is the result of spending lots of time with him. It comes from listening to him so much that his voice and his truth are readily recognizable, and we begin to screen out all that is not true and any voice that is suggesting things contrary to what the Shepherd has said.

Some of the most discerning people I know when it comes

to recognizing the voice of the Shepherd and the voice of the enemy live in parts of the world where formal theological education is not readily available. This does not keep them from knowing the Shepherd, however. Even in the West, discernment is not in direct relation to education. It is always in relation to the intimacy of one's relationship with the Shepherd.

The idea behind the term *self-control* is relevant here. The Greek word is translated "sober" in the King James Bible, and that is an accurate, literal translation. The word can mean not intoxicated with wine or strong drink. In the New Testament, however, it is almost always used as a figure of speech to indicate not intoxicated with ideas and things of the world. A self-controlled person has heeded Paul's admonition to "stop being conformed to this world, but be transformed by the renewing of your mind" (Rom 12:2, author's translation). As Phillips paraphrases Paul, "Don't let the world around you squeeze you into its own mold, but let God remold your minds from within." A self-controlled person is one whose thinking is being shaped by God's truth and not by the prevailing culture in which that person lives.

Our culture tells us that spirits are not very important parts of our world. Cause-effect relationships are almost always thought to be explainable in scientific, biochemical terms or with the logical thought of fallen human nature. Higher education has given little thought to the reality of the spiritual world. Western rationalism and naturalism pervade our educational system and therefore are absorbed by students without our realizing what is happening. We begin to make faulty presuppositions about life because we have not examined those presuppositions. Self-controlled persons have learned to ask the right questions based on their relationship with God and on their knowledge of what he has said is true.

This means, on the one hand, that they will not live in fear of this spiritual enemy, because the Scriptures are clear that he has been defeated by Christ through the cross and the resurrection and that victory is available to us as God's children. On the other hand, they will not just ignore this enemy, but will "resist him, standing firm in the faith" (1 Pt 5:9)—the faith that in Christ we are "more than conquerors" (Rom 8:37).

Know God, but Know Your Enemy, Too

Our first priority is to know God, but if we are really at war with a clever, experienced enemy, we need to know as much as we can about him. One of the first laws of warfare—any kind of warfare—is to know your enemy. Paul told the Corinthians that he was "not unaware of his [Satan's] schemes" (2 Cor 2:11). He was not unaware of how Satan thought, and the Corinthians would have picked this up from a play on words in the language in which they read the letter. The word for *unaware* and the word for *schemes* are built on the same root word, which is the word for *mind*. Not to know how your enemy thinks and how he acts is to give the enemy a strategic advantage over you. This is why governments develop very extensive intelligence-gathering programs. In order to protect themselves, they want to know as much as they can about their enemy or even a potential enemy.

During the Second World War the unit with which I served was assigned at one point to positions facing what was known as the Siegfried line. The Siegfried line was a set of elaborate defensive fortifications facing Germany's border with France. To simply look out over the landscape, one would have had no idea that that kind of defensive structure existed. However, we knew that what appeared to be an innocent-looking farm building was in reality a well-camouflaged concrete bunker housing heavy artillery. To attack a few enemy soldiers in a farm building we would have sent out an infantry squad armed with rifles and hand grenades. To attack heavy fortifications, we called for the Air Force to prepare the way. Knowing our enemy made all the difference.

More recently the United States was involved in the Persian Gulf War. Again, because of effective intelligence-gathering we knew where the enemy had its best troops, tank traps, and minefields. The ignore-the-enemy philosophy would have said, "We have the biggest, best army in the world, the most sophisticated weapons, the smartest bombs. Let's just go in and wipe them out." That would have led to a frontal attack right into the heart of the enemy's defenses. But because we knew the enemy—knew how he thought—we could outflank his defenses and save much suffering and many lives.

Again, this does not mean that we are enemy-centered in our thinking. It doesn't take that kind of concentrated attention to know how he operates. But if we don't know his tactics, we give him a tactical advantage over us. God said through Hosea, "My people are destroyed from lack of knowledge" (Hos 4:6). That lack of knowledge is often ignorance of God's Word and of his directions for how we are to live, but it applies as well to being ignorant of his warnings about our enemy. Most believers would not be able to say with Paul, "We are not ignorant of Satan's schemes."

The Bible itself gives us the balance we need. Christ is the focus of Scripture. There are no long passages on demonology. Therefore our primary focus should be on knowing God and his ways. If we know the truth, then we can easily detect the deceptions of the father of lies. God didn't reveal Satan's ways or assignments in detail, because they change. Christ is *the* way, but Satan has many ways. Jesus is the truth; Satan is the father of lies.

Federal agents don't study counterfeit money. They study the real thing, in order to detect the counterfeit. To protect the public, however, they know how counterfeiters work. In the same way, the Scriptures do not give us a nice, neat organizational chart of the satanic realm. But they do affirm the reality of this enemy and provide the instruction we need to live in victory over him. Satan and demons played a very significant role in the teaching and ministry of Jesus. He certainly did not ignore this enemy, and neither should we.

We are never told that we will not have to fight. On the contrary, we are assured that we will. That is why we need to be *self-controlled and alert* and ready to resist *standing firm in the faith* (see Jas 4:7; 1 Pt 5:8, 9). We cannot exercise faith in what we do not know or really believe.

We do not fight in this war to determine who will win. That was settled once and for all at the Crucifixion and the Resurrection (see Col 2:15; Heb 2:14-15). But we are called on to appropriate that victory and to use the resources provided for us by the Captain of our salvation until he calls us home or until the enemy is finally consigned to his final destiny—the lake of fire.

So, What Am I Afraid Of?

If Christ has really conquered Satan, and if we, as God's children, participate in that victory, why do we so often recoil in fear from the very thought of Satan and demons? Why do we try to escape the battle by denying that it exists?

Some people excuse themselves from active resistance by supposing that only a few are called to resist the enemy and that they are given a special gift to do so. The Scriptures do not speak of any such gift. All Christians are to wear the armor and use the weapons of this warfare. All Christians are to submit to God and resist the enemy.

When people hear that we (both Neil and Tim) were on the faculty at leading evangelical seminaries, they often ask what our faculty colleagues thought about our teaching and practice in this area. Most appreciate the need for balanced biblical instruction but are glad they don't have to do it. Some don't want to think about it. For others, it is not academically credible, and some are actually afraid to deal with it. Yes, there can be a fear of involvement with this enemy even among those who would seem to have the most complete biblical knowledge on the subject.

The problem is, as we have already noted, that our faith is often formal but not functional. We know truth in our heads, but it does not get to our hearts, from which come the issues of life (see Prv 4:23). Theological knowledge, even orthodox theological knowledge, does not necessarily translate into practical application in daily life. This was evident in the life of Israel in the Old Testament. God said through the prophet, "These people come near to me with their mouth and honor me with their lips, but their hearts are far from me" (Is 29:13). Jesus said of the religious leaders of his day who could quote the law and the prophets that they were like tombs that looked good on the outside but inside were full of dead bones (see Mt 23:27). Jesus insisted that "by their fruit you will recognize them" (Mt 7:16). Paul put it very clearly to the Corinthians: "The kingdom of God does not consist in words (*logos*), but in power" (1 Cor 4:20). Concerning this verse John Calvin said, "For how small an affair is it for any one to have skill to prate eloquently, while he has nothing but empty tinkling."[2]

Sometimes when a person challenges me about including demonic activity in dealing with problems people bring to me, I say, "OK. Let me bring to you the next difficult case I have which involves such problems, and you can show me how you would minister to them." That is not usually what they have in mind. I discovered early in my experience that it was much easier to study about this subject and even to teach about it than it was to practice it.

Satan knows this, and he derives special pleasure when Christians say by their actions that they are afraid of him. Satan should be running from the Christian, not the Christian from Satan. Unfortunately, this enemy has been able to use fear to take many soldiers out of the battle. The fear of God—not the fear of the devil—is the beginning of wisdom.[3]

A man who came for counsel told me that he had been in Bible college, studying to be a missionary, when his children began to have nighttime disturbances which he understood to be demonic. He also assumed, probably correctly, that the attacks were being provoked by his commitment to missionary service. He said, "I don't want my children going through this, so I'm getting out." He left school and gave up his call to ministry. My response to him was, "You think you have put your children in a safe place. You have probably put them in the most dangerous place in the world. You have said to Satan, 'I don't know a power stronger than yours. So, if you leave my children alone, I will leave you alone.'" Satan will shake hands on an agreement like that every time. He loves to hear Christians express that kind of fear. Fear of anything or anyone other than God is inconsistent with a genuine faith in God. The problem with such a deal is that Satan is a liar. He has no intention of living up to his end of such a bargain.

A pastor was counseling a person who began to manifest demonic control, evidenced by supernatural strength. This produced fear in the pastor, and his response was to back off and say to himself, "I'll let someone else deal with things like this." Thus, fear of Satan caused one more servant of the Lord to withdraw from the heat of the battle and to cease to be of real help to those suffering from Satan's attacks.

The problem is not really the fear. Fear is a normal response. We just should not let fear control us. We should choose to act in faith on the victory that has been won for us at the cross. "For God did not give us a spirit of timidity, but a spirit of power, of love and of self-discipline" (2 Tm 1:7).

A model for this is found in the experience of Joshua, when God commissioned him to lead the people of Israel into the Promised Land. God told Joshua to "be strong and very courageous" (Jos 1:6-7, 9). He said it not just once, but three times. Why did Joshua need to be courageous? Because the conquest of Canaan was not going to be easy. There were still giants in the land, the same giants seen by the spies forty years before. Joshua, in fact, had been one of those spies, so he knew about the giants and the double-walled cities.

Courage is not the absence of fear. Courage is resolute action in the presence of fear. There is no need for courage if there is no fear involved. That is why Satan is the source of discouragement. He does not want us to act with courage, so he discourages us. God is the encourager. He wants us to act with courage, so he en-courages us. And God has provided the basis on which we can act with courage. It is not just a matter of "whistling in the dark." It is a decision to act on the basis of who God is and what he has done rather than on the basis of a human perspective on the circumstances.

Still a Reluctant Warrior?

So, are your authors still reluctant warriors? In one sense, yes. We don't enjoy being involved in a battle, even though we are assured of victory. But as we learned about spiritual warfare, it seemed essential to teach theological students, who were preparing for pastoral or missionary service, how to fight this war. For this reason we introduced courses to do just that. One of the rewards of our teaching has been to meet graduates all over the world who have told us that our course on this subject was one of the most important ones they ever took.

Not only ministers and missionaries need to know how to fight, however. Every believer will face the same spiritual enemy, and we should not allow Satan to intimidate us and cause us to recoil from the battle. Until Christ returns, the battle will go on, but we are more than conquerors through him who loved us (see Rom 8:37), and we should live in that victory.

TWO

Is This Spiritual Warfare or Plain Old Trouble?

We live in a day of shortcuts and quick fixes—fast-food restaurants, box mixes, TV dinners, automatic teller machines, over-the-counter remedies, drive-up pharmacies, and, of course, the Internet. We of the older generation remember when most meals were prepared from scratch, when woodwork was done entirely with hand tools, when banking was done with a banker rather than a machine, when there were telephone operators instead of answering machines, and when it was not unusual to walk to work or to school.

In the fast-paced world of the twenty-first century, it is very tempting to try to find a shortcut or quick fix for our personal and spiritual problems. Without minimizing the possibility of God intervening in our lives at times of special need with his own miraculous "quick fix," it is safe to say that he usually expects us to use the resources he has given us to work through the problems of life. He made us in his image, with the ability to think, feel, and make decisions, and he encourages us to use those abilities.

Sometimes well-meaning Christians suggest that we should expect God to make all the decisions for us. We are told, "Get out of the driver's seat, and let the Lord take over." While there is an element of truth to that statement, this isn't the way it works. The better picture is that of a young man at the helm of a ship, the Lord standing beside him as a mentor with his hand on his shoulder. There are indeed some things that only God can do—things like creating something out of nothing, sustaining the universe with the word of his power, defining truth, and providing redemption for fallen man. There are some things, however, that God has equipped us to do, and he will not do those things for us. He will be there to help us and to mentor us, but he will not excuse us from using our minds.

He does not fill our minds with a knowledge of his Word. We have to read it, study it, memorize it, meditate on it, and obey it. We have to put on the armor that he has provided for us. We have to meet the changing circumstances of our lives with the resources that are available to us as children whom he loves. We have to use our ability to make decisions. He will help us with the process and correct us when we make bad decisions, but he will never tell us to be passive, either mentally or volitionally.

We live in a fallen world, and our Lord has told us very clearly that "in this world you will have trouble." Fortunately for us, the verse does not end there. Jesus goes on to say, "but take heart! I have overcome the world" (Jn 16:33). The promise of victory, however, does not excuse us from the trouble. It is similar to what we hear God tell his people in the Old Testament: "When you pass through the waters, I will be with you; and when you pass through the rivers, they will not sweep over you. When you walk through the fire, you will not be burned; the flames will not set you ablaze" (Is 43:2). God's people were not promised that they would not go through the floods and the fire. They were simply given the assurance that God would be with them at such times.

So today, we have to expect that we will face difficult situations. This was so even for Jesus: "although he was a son, he learned obedience from what he suffered" (Heb 5:8). Times of trouble and suffering are not all the work of Satan, at least in a direct sense. He is ultimately the source of all that is evil, but although he introduced the corrupting influences into the world, he does not need to be there recreating the evil each time it appears. Let's not give him more credit or more attention than he deserves, and let's not excuse ourselves from doing the things that God has commissioned us to do.

One of those things is to be self-controlled in the use of our minds. God expects us to use our minds to think and our wills to make decisions. He does not say that if we just trust him enough, he will make the decisions for us. On the contrary, he encourages us to use the qualities that reflect his image in us, and those qualities include our minds and our wills. This is not to say that God does not guide us. He does, but he does not reward intellectual laziness. That is poor stewardship of the gift of intelligence he has given us. We noted this truth in chapter one when we heard both Peter and Paul telling us to be "self-controlled and alert."

It should be noted here that mental passivity is not only poor stewardship of the minds God has given to us, it is also one of the most dangerous things we can do, spiritually. It opens us to Satan's deception.

In our quest for quick fixes, however, we may revert to the idea that if we can just locate the right demon to exorcise, we can solve almost any problem. While it is true that there is some spiritual dimension to all human predicaments, it is seldom true that our problem is simply a matter of dealing with a demon.

We have had people ask us if we do exorcisms, because, they have said, they had a demon they wanted to get rid of. The standard answer to such people is: "I have only Christian answers to human problems. If you are interested in seeking God's answers for your life, I am interested in helping you. But if you simply want to get rid of a demon so that you can get on with your own agenda for your life, I cannot promise you any help."

What Is Spiritual Warfare?

If spiritual warfare is not just going around rebuking the devil and getting rid of demons, what is it? The primary battle is between the kingdom of darkness and the kingdom of God, between the Antichrist and the Christ, between the father of lies and the Spirit of truth; and we are in that battle whether we like it or not. The primary location of that battle is our minds. Either we believe the lies that keep us in bondage or we believe the truth that sets us free. So, we define spiritual warfare as the battle for the mind.

Our abilities to think, feel, and make decisions (our minds, emotions, and wills) are intricately linked together. They interact in many ways. Yet it is safe to say that everything begins with the mind. Our thoughts about anything in life are what determine how we feel and how we act. It often appears that emotions are the determining factor, but emotions are only as valid as the truth on which they are based. They are very real and they may lead to significant action, but they all have their roots in what we think about the circumstances of life, whether those thoughts be true or false.

Every action is just a product of our thoughts. "For as he thinks within himself, so he is" (Prv 23:7, NASB). The will can only act on what the mind knows. Wrong information, lack of knowledge, or a faulty belief system can lead to undesirable and even destructive actions. Satan knows this, and this explains why deception is his primary tactic. This is also why, as we noted in chapter one, Peter tells us to "prepare your minds for action; be self-controlled" (1 Pt 1:13). He wants us to understand that if we can win the battle for the mind, we can win the battle against Satan as the deceiver.

The battle for the mind is much more than the struggle to have correct information, however. It is a matter of having a functional faith that is based on truth. It is possible to know the truth intellectually but never apply it to your life. As an example, I was recently talking with a colleague about a book that I had found challenging. My friend knew the author at a personal level, and he said to me, "The only problem is that the author doesn't practice what he writes." This is a very real possibility for all of us. Our knowledge can run well ahead of our functional belief and therefore ahead of how we live.

There is a fundamental difference between the brain and the mind. The brain is an organism that the mind uses. To put it in computer terms, the brain is the hardware, and the mind is the software. One can have a perfectly functioning computer, but if the software program has bugs in it, the results can be disastrous. In computer language, it is "garbage in, garbage out." When I was doing my doctoral work, I stood with a colleague in the computer center of the university and watched a large computer print out complicated statistical correlations for fourteen variables listed down the side of a sheet of paper and twenty-one variables listed across the top. It would have taken months to do all of those mathematical computations by hand. It was a technological marvel (more so in 1967 than in 2000). The only problem was, the answers were all wrong because the computer had not been programmed to handle the data properly. In the same way, the human brain can function only according to how it has been programmed.

If we are not living responsible lives and bearing fruit, then we should take a good look at what we believe and how we think. Life comes down to the principle that if we believe right we will live right, but we need to understand that right belief is more than right knowledge.

Belief Is More Than Profession

There is a saying, "what you do hollers so loud I can't hear what you say." This can be stated as a principle of life: people may not live what they profess, but they will always live what they believe. It is what Jesus meant when he said, "By their fruit you will recognize them" (Mt 7:20).

Our profession of what we believe is often based on truth taught to us by men—things we have read in books or learned in formal study—and there is nothing wrong with that kind of learning. Life-changing belief, however, is based on Spirit-taught truth. Profession is what we know with our brains. Belief is what has found a home in our hearts. Orthodox profession is what enables us to pass theological examinations and even ordination councils. Orthodox belief is what enables us to live to the glory of God. The mind is the battleground. It is where battles are won or lost. That is why Paul says that you can and should be "transformed by the renewing of your mind" (Rom 12:2).

Satan Is the Master Deceiver

Satan does not want that transforming process to take place. He knows that if he can control what we believe, he can control how we live. Demagogues, dictators, and cult leaders have used this tactic for years, but it all began with the devil himself. Paul said that with such evil leaders it is a case of "deceiving and being deceived" (2 Tm 3:13). Satan first deceives the leaders, and they in turn deceive others. Saying they were deceived does not excuse them. We are all responsible for what we think and choose to believe.

When we look at cults and dictatorships from the outside, it seems amazing to us that people can be led into bondage to ideas that are so patently false. But that is the way deceit works. The lie is told so convincingly and so often that it soon seems to be true. It is a time-tested method of controlling people, and none of us is exempt from this possibility.

Consider the fact that this process began in the Garden of Eden—a place where there was no sin, no fallen nature, nothing evil. God created the garden and the people in the garden "very good." Then Satan came on the scene, and notice the approach he used. His aim was to get Adam and Eve to question God's Word. First he tried a big lie. "Did God really say, 'You must not eat from *any* tree in the garden'?" (Gn 3:1, emphasis added). That was obviously false, so Eve told him that they could eat fruit from all the trees of the garden except the one in the middle of the garden; if they ate from that tree they would die. By letting Eve give a correct response to the first question, Satan set her up for where he really wanted to lead her. In Eve's response, she added the words, "You must not touch it." These were not in God's original instructions, and we get into trouble when we add to or subtract from what God says.

Satan's second approach was not a question but a statement. "'You will not surely die,' the serpent said to the woman. 'For God knows that when you eat of it your eyes will be opened, and you will be like God, knowing good and evil'" (Gn 3:4-5). The temptation had two appeals. The first was to suggest that God could not be trusted, that he had told them something that was not true. The second was the appeal to self-interest in suggesting that they could become like God. Satan had become the fiend that he was by trying to be like God (see Is 14:12-15; Mt 4:9; 2 Thes 2:4). Now he was suggesting that possibility to the man and woman God had created in his own image.

It is interesting to speculate on what might have happened had Adam also been involved, and had Adam and Eve talked this over. We are thus introduced to another of Satan's tactics—namely, to isolate us and approach us when we are alone. He will say, "You should be able to handle this by yourself. You shouldn't have to consult God or anyone else." There is just enough truth to such statements to make them enticing, but enough error to make them very dangerous. In any case, Eve did not stop to ask, "Is it true that I cannot trust God? Would God really tell us something that was not true?" The answer seems so obvious that the question hardly needs to be asked, but this calls attention to another of Satan's tactics—a sense of urgency. "Do it right now, without taking time to think it over or to check it out with someone you trust." The really amazing thing is that she did not talk with God about it. He certainly was available.

The crucial issue is, what did Eve believe about God? The minute she entertained the idea that God could not be trusted implicitly, all kinds of things changed for her, and ultimately for Adam and all the rest of us. If God could not be trusted on the issue of the trees of the garden, he could not be trusted for anything. If they needed to use their own judgment about the Tree of Knowledge of Good and Evil, they would need to use their own judgment about everything else as well. That was a staggering prospect—one they were not equipped to handle.[1]

If such deception could happen in a perfect place like the Garden of Eden, it certainly can happen to us in the fallen world in which we live. That is why Paul wrote to the Corinthians, "I am afraid that just as Eve was deceived by the serpent's cunning, your minds may somehow be led astray from your sincere and pure devotion to Christ" (2 Cor 11:3). Even in the church age we are vulnerable. That is why Jesus prayed, "My prayer is not that you take them out of the world but that you protect them from the evil one. They are not of the world, even as I am not of it. Sanctify them by the truth; your word is truth" (Jn 17:15-17). We don't overcome the father of lies by human reasoning or scientific research. We do it with the truth revealed to us in the Bible.

The World, the Flesh, and the Devil

Discussions of spiritual warfare sooner or later get around to asking what the relationship is between the world, the flesh, and the devil. Paul introduces all three elements into his definitive statement about this warfare. He says,

> And you were dead in your trespasses and sins, in which you formerly walked according to the course of this world, according to the prince of the power of the air, of the spirit that is now working in the sons of disobedience. Among them we too all formerly lived in the lusts of our flesh,[2] indulging the desires of the flesh and of the mind, and were by nature children of wrath, even as the rest.
>
> EPHESIANS 2:1-3, NASB

Notice the way Paul links the world, the flesh, and the devil together. He does not suggest that sometimes it is the world we are dealing with, sometimes the flesh, and sometimes the devil. Paul sees them as working so closely together that you really can't understand one without seeing the way it relates to the others. The biblical terms *world (kosmos)* and *flesh (sarx)* can have very different meanings. There is very little ambiguity about Satan's identity in the Bible, but that cannot be said about the definitions of *world* and *flesh*.

The Greek word *kosmos* is used with two very different meanings. Satan is called the "prince" (NIV) or "ruler" (NASB) of this world (*kosmos*) by Jesus (see Jn 12:31; 14:30; 16:11), and we are commanded not to love this world (see 1 Jn 2:15). In a sense Satan created the world that is in view here—the world of fallen human culture—and he is the ruler of that world. This was not part of the world as it came from the creative hand of God, however. God created the world of people and things, and he rules over that creation (see Col 1:17; Heb 1:3). The physical world reveals God's glory, and we are not to reject this. It is part of what God has given us to enjoy (see 1 Tm 6:17), and the world of people created by God is a proper object of our love. God himself "so loved the world [of people] that he gave his one and only Son, that whoever believes in him shall not perish but have eternal life" (Jn 3:16). Thus, the world of people and things as God created it is good. It is not our enemy. It is proper to enjoy God's good creation.

When we speak of the world in the context of the world, the flesh, and the devil, we are talking about a world full of things designed by Satan to tempt us to meet our legitimate human needs in a manner never intended by the Creator. They are the deceptions that Satan has devised to get us to make bad decisions just as Eve did in the garden. With that first bad decision—to listen to Satan rather than to God—a process was begun which has resulted in human cultures that have moved far from the Creator. It began with one person and one decision. It spread to two people, and gradually the process embraced whole nations. So, the *world* today is a complicated, carefully crafted scheme of Satan to lead people away from God and his good purposes for them and into bondage to the lies of an enemy.

This is the world to which we as God's people are no longer to conform (see Rom 12:2). Paul puts this in the form of a strong command that could be translated "Stop conforming to the world!" We have to live our lives in the context of this world, but, as Jesus put it in his high priestly prayer, we are not to be "of the world" (Jn 17:16). In a sense, sanctification is the process of freeing ourselves from and keeping ourselves free from the corrupting influences of the world. That is a key idea in Jesus' prayer for us in John 17.

It is also significant that when Jesus prays about our relationship to the world, he links the world and the devil when he says, "My prayer is not that you take them out of the world but that you protect them from *the evil one*" (Jn 17:15, emphasis added). The idea that sometimes we are just dealing with the world misses the fact that Satan is the one who fabricated this complex of temptations and who is in his own deceptive way pushing us to yield to those temptations. Jesus seemed to assume this relationship when he taught his disciples to pray, "Lead us not into temptation, but deliver us from *the evil one*" (Mt 6:13, emphasis added). We are told to avoid, even to "flee" from places and circumstances that lead to temptation (see 1 Cor 6:18; 1 Tm 6:11; 2 Tm 2:22), but when temptation is happening, we are to resist the enemy (see Eph 6:11; Jas 4:7; 1 Pt 5:9).

Satan is smart enough not to make himself too obvious. He comes to us dressed in his Satan suit only when he wants to scare us, and that is one of his tactics. But more often he comes as an angel of light, or he sends one of his henchmen dressed as a "minister of righteousness" (2 Cor 11:15). Deception is his game. He is a con man.

Paul uses the image of a trap in writing to Timothy. Traps are set to deceive animals into thinking that something good—the bait—is available to them without recognizing that it is attached to a trigger that will spring the trap. Paul says that some people in the church have fallen into the "trap of the devil" and are doing what he wants rather than what God wants. They have fallen for the bait that there is a way other than God's to meet their legitimate needs. Paul makes it clear that the way out of the trap is "the truth" (see 2 Tm 2:25-26). The fact that truth is the way out of the trap implies that lies are the trap or at least the bait in the trap. We are deceived into thinking that we can sin without having to suffer the consequences.

But what about the flesh? Doesn't the Bible say that this is where the battle is really fought? In Galatians chapter five Paul says the struggle is between spirit and flesh, not between spirit and Satan. James tells us that we are drawn away by our own desires, not by a demon (see Jas 1:13-15). Yes, the battle is fought at the level of our flesh; so we need to define *flesh* carefully.[3] The term *flesh*, like the term *world*, can be used in several different ways. A frequently used Greek-to-English dictionary lists eight different meanings for the Greek word *sarx* (flesh).[4]

While this may sound a bit intimidating to one who isn't a Greek scholar, there is a sense in which the meanings all relate to one primary idea. This idea is that we are human beings with physical bodies living in a time-space world. The word *flesh* can mean things related to or part of the body, like flesh and bones, meat, and bodies. Yet we are more than just bodies. We also have personalities that identify us as individuals. Our personalities are made up of our ability to think, feel, and make decisions. The term *flesh* is used to incorporate all of these ideas. In a sense it is simply a way of saying we are human. The problem is, the flesh is weak, and it has been conditioned to operate independently of God. It is hostile to the Spirit of God that is at work in us (see Gal 5:16-17) and that leads us to be totally dependent on God.

We are also spiritual beings who are created in the image of God. This is part of what it is to be human, and all of these human qualities require resources to sustain them. The body needs food and water. As persons or personalities we need to feel significant, secure, and accepted. We need to love and be loved. As spiritual beings we need a relationship with God. It is these needs which are in view when James says that we are drawn away by our own *desires.* We have needs that we desire to have met. This should happen as intended by our Creator. These needs and the desire to meet them were present in the Garden of Eden before sin entered the picture. The desires are not bad. They do not constitute a sinful nature. They were there when God created Adam and Eve.

But Satan has many suggestions as to how those desires can be met in ways contrary to what God originally intended. We have noted how human cultures have tended to degenerate spiritually so that the *world* today is often an enemy of Christian growth and maturity. In a similar manner, our flesh has been programmed to live independently of God. After the Fall, Adam and Eve had lost their relationship with God, so they sought to find identity and purpose for life apart from God.

Learning to live our lives independently of God is what led to the downward course of human culture. Culture is defined most simply as "learned and shared human behavior."[5] Almost everything we humans do is learned. We come into this life with very few instinctive behaviors, in contrast to the animals, who come with a high level of instinctive behavior. Not only are we able to learn, we are able to pass on that learning. Animals can't do that. Dogs can be taught to be seeing-eye dogs for the blind, for example, but no veteran guide dog has ever written a book about it or set up a school to train other guide dogs. Every new generation of dogs starts from scratch. Human beings, however, can write books and teach others what they have learned, and that is what produces what we call culture. Culture is the accumulation of learned ideas and behaviors—good and bad— that are passed down from one generation to the next within societies that share a common heritage. Our modern cultures are the result of learning and cultural borrowing from places and peoples all over the world. It is essentially the part of culture which passes on learned evil that the Bible calls the world.

Most societies place a high priority on having their members conform to the accepted cultural beliefs and practices of those societies. One is accepted and affirmed by a society to the extent that one meets the expectations of that society. A popular contemporary term for this is peer pressure, which can function to promote what is good, but also promote what is evil.

In primitive societies this pressure to conform was fairly uniform throughout the tribe or nation involved. As civilizations have developed and living patterns have become more urban, we have developed many subcultures, and the pressure to conform comes from these subcultures rather than from a unified society as a whole. The modern frustration is "I wish I could be a nonconformist like everyone else." To be more accurate, however, one would need to say, "like everyone else in my subculture." This is the negative connotation of what the Bible calls "the world." It is a world that has unfortunately taken its lead in trying to meet human needs and desires from the god of this world rather than from the one true Creator God. In all too many cases, God is systematically left out of our culture. He is relegated to a heaven that has little contact with earth, or he is replaced by a different god.

Yes, the world tells us that our needs and desires can be met with the counterfeits that Satan has suggested, and people everywhere are frantically trying to meet their needs this way. That was never the intention of our Creator. It is the work of an enemy. When James says we are drawn away by our own *desires* (NIV) or *lusts* (KJV), it is indeed our basic human needs that provide the possibility of our being drawn away, but it is not the needs or desires themselves that are wrong. The word used here is used in other places with a very positive connotation (see Mt 13:17; Lk 22:15; Phil 1:23; 1 Thes 2:17). It has acquired its negative connotation in our minds because of the way we have tried to meet those desires or needs from the supermarket of wrong choices offered by the world. It is not the desires that are wrong, it is the way we have tried to meet them. And just as Jesus linked temptation and the tempter in the prayer he taught his disciples (see Mt 6:9-13), so we need to see that relationship implied in the idea of being *drawn away*. It is Satan who is the mastermind behind that strategy. He is the one who does the drawing away, by suggesting all the deceptive alternatives to us when we try to meet our legitimate needs.

So, in talking about the world, the flesh, and the devil, we need to understand that it is not all one or all the other. Most of the time it is not even mostly one or the other. They work together, and we need a strategy for resistance that takes into account all three without allowing an emphasis on one of them to dominate.[6]

We all have legitimate needs. The question is, are those needs going to be met by the world, the flesh, and the devil, or by Christ, who promises to meet all our needs according to his riches in glory (see Phil 4:19)? I (Neil) wrote *Living Free in Christ*[7] to show how Christ meets our most critical needs, which are the "being" needs—to be accepted, to be secure, and to be significant—as follows:

"In Christ" I am accepted ...

Jn 1:12	I am God's child.
Jn 15:15	I am Christ's friend.
Rom 5:1	I have been justified.
1 Cor 6:17	I am united with the Lord.
1 Cor 6:19-20	I have been bought with a price. I belong to God.
1 Cor 12:27	I am a member of Christ's body.
Eph 1:1	I am a saint.
Eph 1:5	I have been adopted as God's child.
Eph 2:18	I have direct access to God through the Holy Spirit.
Col 1:14	I have been redeemed and forgiven of all my sins.
Col 2:10	I am complete in Christ.

"In Christ" I am secure ...

Rom 8:1-2	I am free forever from condemnation.
Rom 8:28	I am assured that all things work together for good.
Rom 8:31-34	I am free from any condemning charges against me.
Rom 8:35-39	I cannot be separated from the love of God.

2 Cor 1:21-22	I have been established, anointed, and sealed by God.
Phil 1:6	I am confident that the good work God has begun in me will be perfected.
Phil 3:20	I am a citizen of heaven.
Col 3:3	I am hidden with Christ in God.
2 Tm 1:7	I have not been given a spirit of fear, but of power, love, and a sound mind.
Heb 4:16	I can find grace and mercy in time of need.
1 Jn 5:18	I am born of God, and the evil one cannot touch me.

"In Christ" I am significant ...

Mt 5:13-14	I am the salt of the earth.
Jn 15:1,5	I am a branch of the true vine, a channel of his life.
Jn 15:16	I have been chosen and appointed to bear fruit.
Acts 1:8	I am a personal witness of Christ's.
1 Cor 3:16	I am God's temple.
2 Cor 5:17-21	I am a minister of reconciliation for God.
2 Cor 6:1	I am God's coworker (1 Cor 3:9).
Eph 2:6	I am seated with Christ in the heavenly realms.
Eph 2:10	I am God's workmanship.
Eph 3:12	I may approach God with freedom and confidence.
Phil 4:13	I can do all things through Christ who strengthens me.

A friend who was the president of an insurance company was known for his saying: "People change, but not much." His point was that you don't hire people for what they can become, but for what they can do at the time of hiring, because not many people are willing to do what is required to produce change. He made a good point, but people can change. Paul says you can be *"transformed* by the renewing of your minds" (Rom 12:2, emphasis added).

However, one of the problems in fighting this spiritual battle is that the enemy has convinced some people that they can't change. "That's just the way I am," they say. Or, "It works for others, but not for me." Remember, Satan is a deceiver. The idea that you cannot do something God tells you to do has to be a lie from our enemy. God does not command us to do things we cannot do. He does not tell us that we can be victors in most things but that we are powerless against some of the enemy's attacks. He tells us that we are "more than conquerors" (Rom 8:37). Paul doesn't say, "I can do most things through Christ who strengthens me." He says, "I can do everything through him who gives me strength" (Phil 4:13). The problem is that we will always live what we really believe, and if we believe we cannot do something, we won't even try.

Satan has kept many people from spiritual growth and maturity with this tactic. We listen when he suggests things like, "The idea of spiritual victory and fruitfulness is fine for others, but I'm too weak. I just don't have enough faith." "I guess the devil has my number. He knows that I just can't resist in that area," or "I just don't feel that way, and if I do something I don't feel like doing, I am a hypocrite." Notice that Satan will phrase the thoughts as though they were your own. If he can convince you that you really believe something, you will begin to act on that belief.

Perhaps you are asking, at this point, "Are you saying that Satan can put thoughts into my mind? Wouldn't that be like saying, 'The devil made me do it'?"

My answer is, yes, we are saying that Satan can put thoughts into our minds, and no, it is not like saying the devil made you do it. The Scriptures tell us that Satan put thoughts in the mind of David (see 1 Chr 21:1), of Judas (see Jn 13:2), and of Ananias (see Acts 5:3). The devil even put thoughts in Jesus' mind. One day Jesus had this thought in his mind: "If you bow down and worship Satan, he will give you all the kingdoms of the world." What a horrible thing for Jesus to be thinking! Where did that thought come from? It obviously was not from Jesus' own thinking. It came from the devil, who was tempting him.

"But," you say, "wasn't Satan literally present there in the wilderness? Wasn't that different from how Satan tempts us?"

The Bible says that Jesus was "tempted in every way, *just as we are*" (Heb 4:15, emphasis added). The devil is a spiritual being, and Jesus had taken on the form of a man (see Phil 2:7). Satan may have materialized so that he was visible to Jesus. We are not given that kind of detail in the biblical account. Even if he did appear, however, he was still a spiritual being, and the communication was from a spirit to a person. That is the way temptation happens; Jesus was tempted "just the way we are." If it happened to Jesus, you have to believe that it can happen to us.

Being tempted, however, is not sin. We cannot prevent temptation, but we can resist the temptation. That is why it is never correct to say, "The devil made me do it." We are always responsible for what we allow into our minds and for what we do with the stimuli to evil that are all around us in the world.

But to deny that Satan is involved in the process is to fail to deal with one of the critical elements in any temptation.

Of course, it is not really Satan who is doing the tempting. Satan is only one angel—a fallen angel, to be sure. He would like to have us believe that he is omnipresent, like God, but that simply isn't so, and we should never ascribe the attributes of deity to him. He has to depend on his demonic hierarchy to carry out his nefarious schemes. This is what was behind Martin Luther's famous words, "And though this world with devils filled should threaten to undo us, we will not fear, for God hath willed his truth to triumph through us." Satan and his host of fallen angels are everywhere in "the world," but that should not cause us alarm, because God has given us the truth as our primary defense against their deceitful attacks.

It's Both

We all have our share of spiritual conflict and we began this chapter by asking, "Is this spiritual warfare or just plain old trouble?" The answer is, "It's both." They go together. If Satan doesn't cause the trouble, he will try to take advantage of it when it comes to us. Living in a fallen world produces plenty of trouble without Satan starting something new. But he is an opportunist, and he will be on hand to make the trouble seem even worse than it is and to make you feel so much like a victim that you will begin to act like a victim rather than like a victor in Christ.

The battle is for the mind. It is a battle of truth versus lies. If we can win that battle, we can win all the others.

THREE

Toward a Biblical Worldview

Everyone lives by faith. The only difference between Christian and non-Christian faith is the object of our faith. The Christian has chosen to believe God and his Word. However, before we came to Christ, we believed in something or someone else. Even if we have been Christians since childhood, we have developed certain attitudes and beliefs about ourselves and the world in which we live—our worldview. This assimilation happened without our realizing that it was happening. Unless we were reared in a perfect Christian home, there is no way we could have a biblical understanding of the world in which we live.

In his book *The Universe Next Door,* James Sire defines worldview as "a set of presuppositions or assumptions which we hold (consciously or subconsciously) about the basic make-up of the world."[1] Those presuppositions or assumptions act like a filter or set of filters through which we pass all of the input from the world around us in order to give it meaning.[2] As Sire indicates, this often happens at the subconscious level. Most of us are not even conscious of having a worldview, because we have just absorbed it from the culture in which we were reared. It is the climate in which we have grown up, and it has never dawned on us that we should question it. We make very significant judgments about the events in our lives, judgments that may very well be based on a faulty worldview, as far as the Scriptures are concerned. One of the best ways to discover this is to live in a place where the worldview is very different from the one with which you grew up.

For example, I (Tim) went to West Africa as a missionary in 1956. My wife and I served in a typical tribal village. We were the only non-Africans in the village. The tribal people were animists with a strong belief in the spirit world. When people hear this, they sometimes say to us, "I suppose you saw a lot of spiritual warfare out there."

My response is, "No, I didn't. I wouldn't have recognized it if I had seen it." I was the graduate of a fine Christian college and a theological seminary that majored in teaching the Bible. I also had a further graduate degree from a major American university. But in none of this education had anyone helped me understand either worldview as a concept, what my own worldview was, or any concept of the worldview of the people with whom I was to minister. I was a typical Westerner. I was well educated by our Western standards, but even my theological education had not helped me deal with worldviews and especially beliefs about the spirit world.

As a result, when I heard the Africans talk about spirit activity, it passed through a filter in my mind called superstition. That is why I have to say I didn't see a lot of spiritual warfare in Africa. It was not because it was not there. It was because my Western worldview prevented me from recognizing it.

The problem often went well beyond things the Africans said and did. It included the things the missionaries said and did. Even missionaries tended to see all problems as problems with only human dimensions. Spiritual warfare was almost never seen as a possible element in the activities and relationships of missionaries, even though those activities and relationships were often very problematic.

In our Western worldview we tend to assume that a demon cannot do anything to a "good" Christian, and that the best thing to do with Satan and demons is to ignore them. We do this in spite of the fact that the Bible never tells us to ignore the devil; that is just where our Western worldview has led us. The Bible, on the contrary, tells us to resist the devil. The Greek word translated *resist* or *stand against* is the same in Ephesians 6:13, James 4:7, and 1 Peter 5:9, and "good" Christians are not exempt. Even the apostle Paul had a "messenger of Satan, to torment" him (2 Cor 12:7), and Satan "hindered" him from carrying out his plans to visit Thessalonica (1 Thes 2:18, KJV).

Going back to the concept of worldview as a filter, we have to conclude that our Western worldview filters are faulty. If a filter is properly constructed on the basis of biblical teaching and is operating well, we will arrive at valid Christian conclusions about our experiences in the world. If it is not properly constructed or is not functioning well, we will arrive at faulty or even dangerously wrong conclusions about our experiences in the world.

Therefore, the worldview part of our belief system is critically important, and too often the church has given little attention to it. The most logical reason for the church's failure is that Satan has been successful in his deception.

This is a significant part of what Paul had in mind when he wrote to the Romans, "Stop being conformed to this world" (Rom 12:2, literal translation). Being conformed or not conformed to the world includes the things we do and don't do, but it goes way back to the worldview with which we interpret what we experience in the world. This problem of worldview is also involved in Jesus' statement, "You will know the truth, and the truth will set you free" (Jn 8:32).

A Look at Some Worldviews

It may help us to understand what we are talking about if we look at some representative worldviews. People seem to develop a great deal of tolerance for contradiction in their belief systems, and as a result, we seldom find a society where all the people hold exactly the same worldview. This is especially true of those of us who live in the West. A major pollster says that the problem is not that Americans don't believe anything. It is that they believe everything.[3] He is referring to the fact that there is a great deal of tolerance for conflict in professed beliefs. Persons who at one point seem to be very Western and scientific in their outlook will at other times resort to very animistic practices or to profession of Christian faith. It will help to understand the differences in worldview, however, in order to see how the belief systems may be in conflict.

Animism: A World Controlled by Spirits

Animism is probably the most widely held worldview on our planet. It is defined simply as the belief that spiritual power and spirit beings have a role in almost everything that happens in this world.

It is found in its purest form in the preliterate, tribal societies of our world, but some elements of it are also found to significant degrees in most modern societies. Animism is not considered a world religion or a high religion because it has never been formalized as have Christianity, Islam, Judaism, and Hinduism. Because it is found primarily among preliterate societies, it does not have a "holy book," as world religions do. It does not deal extensively with the cosmic issues in religion. It is much more concerned with the practical realities of daily life, and there are many variations from tribe to tribe. There are, however, some general beliefs that are associated with this worldview.

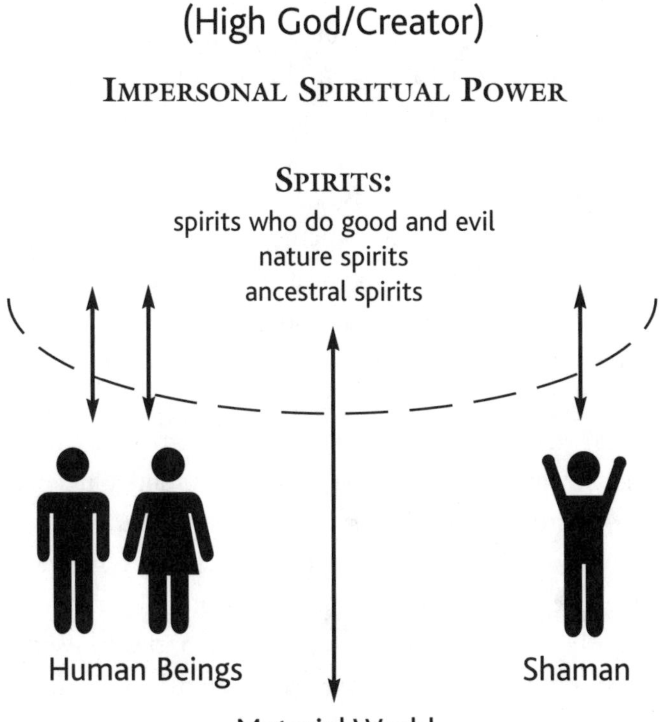

(High God/Creator)

IMPERSONAL SPIRITUAL POWER

SPIRITS:
spirits who do good and evil
nature spirits
ancestral spirits

Human Beings

Shaman

Material World

Figure 1: Animistic Worldview

Most animists believe in a creator or a high god of some kind, but in most instances they see him as being so far removed from them that contact is unlikely, if not impossible. Therefore, our diagram shows him in parentheses way at the top. While he may be referred to in some ceremonies or rituals, he does not play a very significant role in daily life.

Two sources of spiritual power are dominant in the animists' approach to daily life. The first is their belief in an impersonal spiritual power (technically called *mana* in anthropological literature) which is thought to permeate everything in the universe—animal, vegetable, and mineral. The second is spirits of many types.

In some places, especially in the Orient, the impersonal spritual power may be called *god*. This, in turn, may lead to the belief that everyone and everything is part of this impersonal god. More often, however, it is thought to be a power much like electricity, which in itself is neither good nor evil. It is simply there, and it is powerful. Whether it produces good or evil depends on how human beings relate to it. Just as electricity can be generated, raised, or lowered in power, channeled to the place it is needed, and so on, so it is thought that *mana* can be controlled.

In our everyday lives, we all relate to electricity by turning switches on and off, changing light bulbs, and plugging in extension cords, but we also have specialists in dealing with electricity, because if not handled properly, it can harm or even kill you. We love it for its ability to light lights and turn motors, but we fear it because of its power to cause pain or death. We don't call it evil when it shocks us. We recognize that this is just the way electricity is.

The animist sees *mana* in much the same way. It is nonethical and nonmoral. It is just there. Whether it does good or evil depends on which switches we throw and how we handle it. So, just as we use a specialist to handle electrical installations and problems, the animists use a spiritual electrician to handle problems facing them in the spirit realm. This person is called a shaman (also called a witch doctor or a medicine man) and is the expert in dealing with this impersonal spiritual power. All animists relate to *mana* in their daily lives, just as we relate to electricity, but when they want something special done—whether good or evil—they go to the shaman, because he or she knows the special formulas, activities, and words necessary to manipulate this power.

This kind of belief is found in all parts of the world and in the religious practices of those professing to believe the teachings of one of the world religions. In France, for example, there are more magical healers—persons who call on this impersonal spiritual power to help in the healing process—than there are medical doctors. In Thailand, where Buddhism is the dominant religion, a university professor confided to a missionary friend that he did not know a single Thai intellectual who was not also an animist. He said that the president of the university at which he taught regularly consulted the spirits before making major academic decisions.

This leads to the second source of spiritual power for animists—namely, spirit beings with individual identities and functions. They are not amoral, as *mana* is thought to be. They knowingly engage in good or evil actions. They may be thought to be spirits associated with objects in nature; they may be conceived of as the spirits of people who have died; or they may be seen in a whole variety of other ways. (Please note that what animists believe about such spirits may not be true, but that it is the belief system that controls their actions. We always need to remember that Satan is a deceiver and that he will lead people to believe anything that will keep them away from the truth.)

As with *mana*, spirits also are thought to be controllable, to some extent at least, by humans, if the humans know the right things to do, words to say, and objects to use. The control is not absolute, however, and this lack of control causes animists to live in constant fear of displeasing the spirits and thus incurring their wrath. They also fear that an enemy may be using some superior occult skill to direct the power of *mana* or the power of the spirits against them. For the true animist, almost everything in life is related in some way to the spirit world. We could say they ascribe a maximum of causation to the supernatural.

For the animist, therefore, the biblical accounts of the activities of Satan and his corps of demons are readily interpreted through the filter of their worldview. It is important to note that the worldview of the people of biblical times was much closer to animism than it was to our secularized Western worldview.[4]

Western Worldview

There is no one Western worldview. The West has become so multicultural that there is no agreement on belief systems among those who live there. There are, however, some things that can be said about the worldview with which most Westerners have grown up.

Some people in the West deny the existence of a God altogether, while others deny that God created the world. These are critically important worldview assumptions. They are so obviously not biblical that we would recognize them rather readily. However, the worldview that tends to dominate the thinking even of people reared in the church has some serious flaws. It usually includes a Creator God, so most Americans still profess to believe in such a God. Believing in Creation does not guarantee a biblical worldview, however.

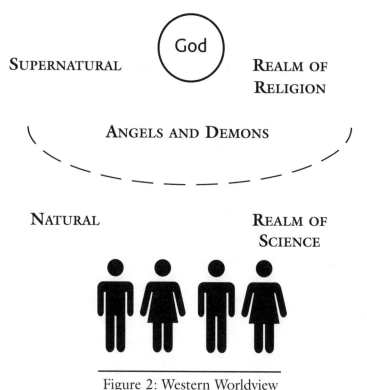

Figure 2: Western Worldview

The Western worldview is generally divided into two functional realms: the supernatural realm and the natural realm. In the supernatural realm we place all spirit beings, including God, angels, and demons, because they are supernatural and do not fit into the natural world that is dominated by scientific thinking. It is assumed that this realm is so far removed from the natural realm that it is like there is a great chasm between them. They not only are separate; they don't even touch. Spiritual issues are considered unnecessary for understanding life; they are therefore optional for eduction. Religion can thus be left out of our schools, it is thought, without losing anything important in the educational process.

The natural realm is thought to be governed by scientific laws. God may have created the world and established the laws which govern it, but he is now seated on his throne in heaven, and he seldom interferes with life on earth. Occasionally we experience a "miracle," but that is the exception, not the rule. Public education in the United States operates on the assumption that religion and science are two different realms which do not interact and should be kept separate. To be more accurate, in public schools in America, the assumption is that Christian beliefs must be kept separate from public education, but other religious beliefs called by different terms may be admitted to the schools. Other religions are treated as parts of culture, but evangelical Christianity is too authoritarian to be compatible with the modern worldview.

On the basis of this worldview, we tend to ask either-or questions like, "Is it a matter of religion or a matter of science?" "Is it a demon or just the flesh?" "Is this a private (things with a spiritual base) or public (things with a scientific or natural base) consideration?" The one I hear most often is, "How do you know whether a person's problem is spiritual or psychological?" In response to this last question, we answer, "We consider that an invalid question based on an invalid worldview." God created me with part of me secular and part of me spiritual. I am a whole person with all my parts intricately related to each other. That includes my body, my soul (psyche), and my spirit. My *psyche* cannot be reduced to something that is explained scientifically. My soul is part of the image of God in me and can only be properly understood in that light. My body, soul, and spirit constantly interact. It is only a perverted Western worldview that has tried to explain life without reference to God and the reality of the spirit world.

A wrong worldview will lead to wrong conclusions about our lives and the world we live in. Trying to resolve physical problems by spiritual means is not always the best approach, although God can miraculously intervene. Trying to resolve spiritual problems by physical means will never work. Taking a pill to help cure your body may be commendable, but taking a pill to cure the soul is deplorable. A biblical worldview will see the need for the pastor as well as the doctor.

If you go back about three hundred years in Western culture, you will find that the worldview was quite different. In western European universities it was assumed that theology was "the queen of the sciences." Everything was tested by its agreement with truth revealed in the Bible, whereas today the concept of revealed truth is not even admissible in most university settings. It was assumed back then that this is a created world and that God speaks both through his creation and through his revealed Word. The physical world could be properly understood only when it was seen as God's work and as a part of his revelation to us.

With the Enlightenment came strong philosophical voices denying revelation. They said man did not get significance from a relationship to some supernatural person or power but from the fact that he was a reasoning being. Then the scientific revolution added the concept that the scientific method was the only reliable method of finding truth, and divine revelation was secondary or insignificant. Still later the theory of evolution was added to this philosophical mix, and, since the world was assumed to have evolved rather than been created, we could no longer see it as a channel of God's revelation.

This Enlightenment worldview not only eliminated God

from any functional relationship to life on earth, it also eliminated the idea of angels and demons. Such spirit beings had no place in the thinking of Enlightenment society. This worldview became so pervasive in the West that even theologians and pastors were influenced by it. John W. Montgomery, a well-known theologian, says,

> The modern clergyman, operating in a world that has been ideologically post-Christian since the 18th century Enlightenment, has been trained to think along maximally secular lines. Under fire from the guns of unbelief, caricatured as a naïve supernaturalist in an age when the supernatural is being progressively eliminated as a meaningful explanatory construct, ... the contemporary minister has tried to get rid of all unnecessary supernatural baggage so as to travel lighter and reduce his credibility gap. At very worst, the result has been a "more secular than thou" stance.... Demonology was the first piece of 'supernatural baggage' to be jettisoned in the reconstruction of theology in the modern age.[5]

With the penetration of this secularized Western worldview into the church, it is no wonder that spiritual warfare is seldom addressed in the church today, or even in Christian higher education.[6] It is also clear why worldview is such a crucial topic in discussing spiritual warfare.

The Biblical Worldview

The worldviews of "the nations" in the Old Testament and of the Greek and Roman cultures in the New Testament are a combination of animism and polytheism (belief in many gods), so Israel and the early church were always being challenged to wrong belief and practice. The worldview taught by the prophets and apostles, however, is the one we need to adopt.

The biblical worldview has three functional realms: the realm of God or deity, the realm of angels, and the realm of people and things.[7] It is important to state that when we talk about these realms, we are not talking about spatial realms but realms of being. God is certainly not limited to a spatial realm far away in outer space. He is present everywhere in his creation. But God is the one being in the realm of deity—not God and angels, and certainly not God and Satan. Some Christians have such fear of Satan that they ascribe godlike qualities to him. Some have even confessed that they see him as the counterpart of God—God being the eternal good and Satan the eternal evil. Satan isn't the eternal anything. He is a fallen angel and should never have the attributes of deity ascribed to him.

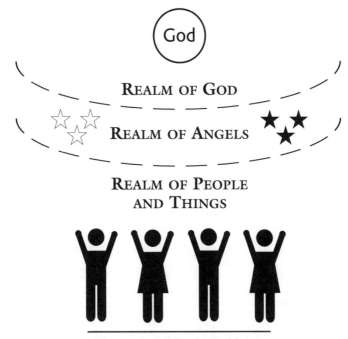

Figure 3: Biblical Worldview

The realm of angels is the one Westerners have problems with. They prefer not to see spirit beings as functional parts of our world, because their existence in our material world is not compatible with Enlightenment thinking and scientific materialism. Hence all spirit beings are assigned to the supernatural realm.

However, as the world came from the creative hand of God, the realm of angels was fully populated. There were various types of angels, including cherubs, seraphs, archangels, principalities, and powers. There are twelve or thirteen terms used in the Bible for the angels, and the angels are seen performing many functions. They worship God in heaven and carry out God's orders in relation to his creation and to people on earth. It was obviously a good arrangement, as it came from the hand of God. God himself pronounced it "very good."

Unfortunately, it did not stay "very good," because one of the highest of the angels decided to lead a rebellion against God and his authority. We do not have a clear narrative account of what happened, but it appears that Lucifer decided that he would like to be a being equal to God. He apparently persuaded a whole group of the angels to join him in his revolt. We often refer to them as "fallen angels."[1] We see Satan trying to act like God when he tempted Jesus to fall down and worship him (Lk 4:5-7). Paul tells us that at the end of this age he will come in "the man of sin" and exalt "himself over everything that is called God or is worshiped, and even set himself up in God's temple, proclaiming himself to be God" (2 Thes 2:3-4).

1. Revelation 12:4 says that the tail of the dragon swept a third of the stars out of the sky. This is often thought to refer to the angels who joined in his rebellion referred to in Matthew 25:4, 2 Peter 2:4, and Jude 9. We have chosen to use stars as symbols for angels in Figure 3.

He seems to have one great ambition—to be God, or at least to be like God. He knows now that he will never make that goal (see Rv 12:12), so he is committed to opposing all of God's purposes for the rest of his creation.

What Is the Big Issue?

Satan's primary issue with God seems to be the fact that God has all the glory and he has none. His objective now is to grab glory himself and to deprive God of his. He can't launch a frontal attack on the throne of God, but he can get some measure of satisfaction by causing God's people on earth to stumble and therefore fail to glorify God in their bodies. In the Ten Commandments, God commanded Israel, as his chosen people, not to bear the name of Yahweh in vain (see Ex 20:7). We have usually understood this to mean that we should not use the Lord's name as a curse or in profanity. That is certainly part of the meaning, but God was also talking about his people being called the children of God and then not living in a way that would bring glory to him. If we profess Christ but live for the devil, it destroys our witness and brings shame to God's name.

Israel lived in the midst of the "nations"—the Gentiles, those who did not know the God of Israel. The primary evangelistic methodology at that time was for Israel to live in such obedience to and trust in God that God could reveal himself through Israel to the other nations. The Gentiles would look on Israel and say, "We don't know a God like yours." But when Israel sinned and did not live to the glory of God, that message was not conveyed, and Israel bore the name "children of God" in vain.

In the New Testament, Paul tells us that "whether you eat or drink or *whatever* you do, do it all for the glory of God" (1 Cor 10:31, emphasis added). To call ourselves children of God and then not to live in a way that reflects his glory is to bear the Lord's name in vain and to give Satan satisfaction. The idea of pleasing Satan rather than God should be enough motivation for us to live God-honoring lives.

So, the major thrust of spiritual warfare is not the more sensational types of demonic manifestations. The primary battle is over control of our daily lives. The problem is that if our worldview does not include a correct view of God and does not see Satan as a functional part of this struggle, we will wrestle with flesh and blood and forget we are also spiritual beings wrestling with principalities and powers (see Eph 6:12).

The Danger of Syncretism

Unless one's worldview is brought into line with the worldview of the Bible at the time of conversion or in the early stages of discipleship, a syncretism is very apt to develop. Syncretism is a technical term for what results when people say they believe one thing but demonstrate by their behavior that they really believe something quite different, or when they say they believe things that are contradictory. For example, a Christian in an animistic society was approached by another Christian because of some sin in the life of the first man. Instead of thanking his friend and dealing with the sin, the man became very angry. He said, "I will never forgive you for this. I'll tell the church that I do, because I know I am supposed to forgive; but Ingos (his tribe) don't forgive!" He was saying that he professed Christianity with Christ as Savior and Lord and the Bible as the final authority in faith and life, but in reality his actions demonstrated that he placed his tribal beliefs above those of the Scriptures. His cultural worldview took precedence over his biblical worldview.

We can't fully understand the Bible and its message without coming to terms with the warfare worldview that it presents. By a warfare worldview we mean that the cosmic battle between God and the gods in the Old Testament and between the kingdom of God and the kingdom of Satan in the New Testament is a real battle. God in his sovereignty has guaranteed the outcome of the war, but the battles we fight from day to day require us to use the minds and wills he has given us and to utilize the armor and the weapons he provides.

A biblical worldview takes into account the sovereignty of God. He is the ultimate source of power in this universe. He is, in fact, the only source of power. He has delegated power to angels and to men, but he is the source of that power. Both angels and men may misuse the power they have been given, but they do not produce power apart from the creative act of God.

Many worldviews include other sources of power—an impersonal kind of power, various kinds of spirits, or even man as his own god. In animism, if there is a belief in a god, he is essentially powerless—certainly not sovereign. In the West, God may be affirmed but is too often treated like a deistic God—One who created the world but now sits on his throne in heaven and doesn't interfere with the operation of the world. Unless God is seen as the only legitimate source of power, however, we will continue to look to other sources for the power we need or at least think we need. For example, in an East African country, an evangelical mission agency was ready to turn over leadership of the church they had planted to African leaders. Two men were seen as candidates for the position. One of them went to a witch doctor to secure a charm to enhance his chances of being chosen leader of the church. What was this man saying about his real belief system? He was saying, "I'm not sure about the power of God, but I really believe in the power of the witch doctor, so I am going to cover all the bases." This is syncretism at its worst—at the leadership level. It was obvious that the candidate for bishop of his church had not adopted a worldview in which God is sovereign as part of his conversion to Christianity.

While we decry that kind of syncretism in Africa, we have the same problem in the West. It is just that for us it often comes from acting on the secularized worldview of our Western culture rather than on the worldview of the Scriptures. We say we believe the Bible, but we also read the horoscope and call the psychic hotline. This is why we have chosen to devote a chapter to this critical subject.

Conclusion

It is clear that our worldview will have a great deal to do with how we understand spiritual warfare. It is also clear that the biblical worldview is essential if we are to live to the glory of God and to be "more than conquerors" in Christ. Paul shows the contrast between the two opposing worldviews and warns us against syncretism in Colossians 2:8-10:

See to it that no one takes you captive through hollow and

deceptive philosophy, which depends on human tradition and the basic principles of this world rather than on Christ. For in Christ all the fullness of the Deity lives in bodily form, and you have been given fullness in Christ, who is the head over every power and authority.

This is also what Paul had in mind when he commands us, "Do not conform any longer to the pattern of this world, but be transformed by the renewing of your mind" (Rom 12:2). A biblical worldview is essential for a renewed mind. It is also a necessary ingredient in understanding spiritual warfare and in fighting the battles victoriously.

■■■■■■■■■■■■■■■■■■■■■■■■■■■■■■

FOUR

More Than Technique

I n most wars there is an element of suspense or uncertainty. Who will win is not often predetermined—at least not from the standpoint of the people involved.

This War Has Already Been Won

A unique thing about the spiritual warfare in which we are involved is that we already know how the war will turn out. We need to distinguish between the battles that make up the war and the war itself. We may lose some battles, but the outcome of the war is no longer in doubt. Christ determined that when he paid the penalty for our sin at the cross and when he conquered death by rising from the tomb. The writer to the Hebrews puts it this way:

> Since the children [that's you and me] have flesh and blood, he too shared in their humanity so that *by his death he might destroy him who holds the power of death*—that is, the devil— and free those who all their lives were held in slavery by their fear of death.
>
> HEBREWS 2:14-15, emphasis added

We can even say that we have all the resources we need to win every battle. The only question is whether or not we will fight the battle the Lord's way, using the weapons, armor, and strategy that come from him. This principle is illustrated in the battles Israel fought with their enemies in the Old Testament. When they were acting in faith and obedience, they always won, no matter how lopsided the military odds seemed to be. Gideon is a great example of this. When the angel of the Lord went to call Gideon to be the leader of the forces of Israel, Gideon said, "I am the least member of my family, and my family is the weakest in the whole tribe of Manasseh." The angel reminded him that the issue was not who *he* was but who *God* is. "Do things God's way," the angel prompted, "and God will be responsible for the results. "Gideon chose to obey, and with three hundred men armed only with torches, clay pots, and trumpets they routed the whole army of the Midianites (see Jgs 6–7).

When Israel did not bother to consult God before a battle and tried to figure things out for themselves, they always lost. At Ai, for example, they did their demographic study and made their strategy decision based on their own evaluation of the situation. Much to their surprise and consternation, they were soundly defeated by the men of the little village of Ai. In fact, thirty-six Israelite families were without husbands and fathers after that abortive battle. They did things their way, apparently without even praying about it, and they got what their way could produce (see Jos 7–8).

This principle continues to operate in the warfare in which we are engaged today. Do things God's way, and God will be responsible for the results. Do things our way, and we must be responsible for the results.

So, if the outcome of the battle we are called on to fight depends on our doing things God's way, we need to make certain that our relationship with the Lord is a functional one and that it is up-to-date.[1] We also need to be certain that we are in touch with the Lord through a knowledge of his Word and a meaningful prayer life.

Is It Magic or Faith?

Spiritual warfare is not just a question of technique—saying the right words, doing the right things, using the right objects, praying the right prayers. This is magical thinking. Those who practice magic assume that there is a power that can be manipulated by using the right techniques. That, however, is not Christianity. We cannot manipulate God.

In our technological age, we may not think of this in terms of magic, but we have become a people of handbooks and manuals. Since we are dealing with physical objects, we need to know how to put them together and make them work. We receive manuals with almost every appliance, vehicle, and piece of electrical goods we buy. We even get manuals with toys! Yet God does not use manuals to enable us to manipulate spiritual power. The Bible is sometimes compared to the instruction books we get with things, but there is a difference. Instruction books tell us how to handle an object. The Bible tells us how to relate to the Creator of the object.

If it had been Americans fighting the battle of Jericho, when it was all over we would have appointed a task force to write a manual on "How to Take a Double-Walled City." The only problem is that if such a manual had been written based on the experience at Jericho, it would never have been useful, because God made his people come back to him personally for new instructions for every new battle. This is not to say that we cannot learn from our participation in the battle, but it is to say that our confidence cannot be in having a manual that tells us which techniques to use to win our battle with Satan. It is not a matter of technique but of relationships. Our relationship with our Lord is basic to understanding and dealing with our relationship with our enemy. With that in mind, let's look at those relationships.

Some Warfare Relationships

The biblical worldview we developed in the last chapter provides a background for looking at some of the key relationships in our spiritual warfare. Beginning with the concept of the three functional realms of being—God, angels, and people—we first add the fact that there are believers and unbelievers in the realm of people. These two groups are separated by the cross. Believers are those who have exercised saving faith in the fact that Christ bore the penalty for all their sin when he died in their place on the cross. Unbelievers are those who have not done this. The possibility of entering into this relationship with God is offered to us through his "amazing grace." He planned for this before he even created us (see Eph 1:4-5), and he initiated the action that made it possible (see Rv 13:8). It is made effective in our lives as we receive it by faith (see Eph 2:8-9). That act of faith brings us into a whole new relationship with God, and we will be looking at that relationship. First, however, we need to take a brief look at the relationship between Satan and both the unbelievers and the believers as we find this explained in the Bible.

Satan's Relationship to the Unbeliever

We have already noted that Satan's primary tactic is deception. We are told in Revelation 12:9 that he is the one who "deceives the whole world" (NKJV) or who "leads the whole world astray" (NIV). He uses deception as the means of control over people. John tells us that "the whole world is under the control of the evil one" (1 Jn 5:19). Paul says that the unsaved person follows "the ways of this world and of the ruler of the kingdom of the air" (Eph 2:2).

Deception is a very clever and effective tactic, because if someone attacks you, you know it. You can defend yourself, whether the attack is verbal or physical. If someone tempts you, you know it. You have a choice to make. But if someone deceives you, you don't know it. If you knew it you wouldn't be deceived. You accept what is being told to you as the truth and proceed to act on it.

We noted in the last chapter that demagogues, dictators, and cult leaders have used this strategy from the time Satan introduced it in the Garden of Eden. People have been led to do many bizarre things when they have fallen for the deception. Satan has had many years of experience to develop his ability to tell lies so cleverly that we don't even think about the possibility that what he says may be a lie. At times we may recognize that we have been deceived, but our pride keeps us from admitting it.

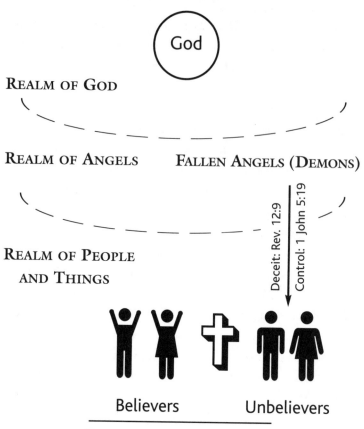

Figure 4: Satan and Unbelievers

Yes, deception is an effective means of control. Actually Satan has to tell unbelievers only one lie to keep them under his control. That lie is that there is a way to find true life other than through the cross of Christ. Satan is the enemy of the cross. It was at the cross that he was disarmed (see Col 2:15) and ultimately destroyed (see Heb 2:14-15). Satan is not the enemy of religion. He will suggest any kind of a religious idea if he thinks he can use it to keep people from the cross.

Paul tells us that "the god of this age has blinded the minds of unbelievers, so that they cannot see the light of the gospel of the glory of Christ, who is the image of God" (2 Cor 4:4). A deceived person believes a lie and is thus blind to the truth. Satan doesn't care how close you come to the truth—as long as you miss it. This is why one of his favorite disguises is to appear as an angel of light or as a servant of righteousness (see 2 Cor 11:13-15). When people think they are being very religious in what they believe or what they do, they assume that they must be right. "Just so you are sincere," the enemy will say. "Religion is a very personal thing. You have to discover what is true for you."

Even a hasty survey of the world indicates that he has been very successful at this. One can find religious belief systems of all kinds, and the prevailing thought of contemporary culture is that any one of them will get you to your desired goal. It is socially acceptable today to talk about spirituality, but it is not politically correct to believe that God has spoken authoritatively in the Scriptures and in the Person of his Son. So it is still true that the whole unbelieving world "is under the control of the evil one" (1 Jn 5:19), kept there with the simple device of a lie.

Satan's Relationship to the Believer

Since our concern in this book is with the spiritual warfare of the believer, we turn now to a consideration of the relationship between Satan and the believer.

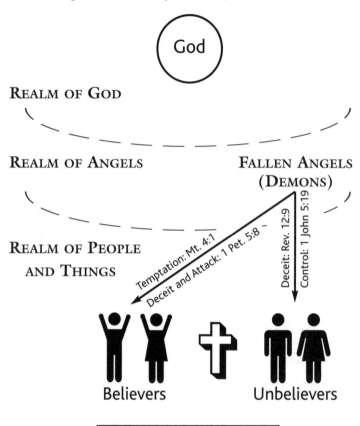

Figure 5: Satan's Relationship to the Believer

When a person comes to the cross and moves from Satan's camp into God's camp, a lot of things change. Paul says that such a person becomes "a new creation; the old has gone, the new has come!" (2 Cor 5:17). One thing that doesn't change is Satan's tactic. He is still the liar and deceiver he has always been (see Jn 8:44; Rv 12:9). We do not become immune to his deceit simply by becoming followers of Christ. In fact, we will discover that he steps up his attacks considerably, because now we have the capacity to live to the glory of God (see 1 Cor 10:31), and we have the potential to help people move from Satan's kingdom into God's kingdom. He is therefore more concerned with neutralizing the child of God than with harassing those who are already in his own kingdom.

We use the term *neutralize* intentionally. Satan knows that he is not going to get many believers to renounce their faith and turn away from the Lord. But he also knows that he can deceive us to the extent that we will not live our Christian lives in a way that will bring glory to God, and we will not resist him "in the faith" (1 Pt 5:9). This has the effect of neutralizing us in the battle. We aren't worshipping him, but we aren't hurting him much either. It may be more comfortable sitting on the sidelines, but it is not the way to fight a war.

When a person begins to get really serious about serving the Lord, the attacks from the enemy can be expected to increase. We could say that the Christian is the devil's target, but those actively involved in ministry are the bull's-eye. Sometimes people ask, "Before I was really sold out to the Lord and seeking to serve him, I didn't have the problems I have now. How come?" The answer is, "Welcome to the war. When you get up on the front lines of battle, you can expect to be shot at."

Suppose that you are an infantryman on the front lines of a military battle and can see the enemy soldiers. There are some with stripes on their sleeves, but there is one with an eagle or even a star on his shoulder. At whom would you choose to shoot first? It only makes sense that if a leader can be taken out of the battle it is going to affect the enemy much more than if a foot soldier is taken out. Satan is not ignorant. He is stupid for rebelling against God, but he knows the strategic persons at whom to shoot in the camp of his enemy.

The problem often is that because of his deceptive tactics, Satan's attacks are not recognized as such. We forget that our struggle is not against flesh and blood, but against principalities and powers. As we noted in the discussion on the world, the flesh, and the devil, it is not correct to see the devil behind every problem, but neither is it correct to not see his involvement in the problem. Many pastors have fallen sexually because they have believed the devil's lie that they would not be tempted in that area. I have seen this happen to colleagues who were very close to me, and they have actually told me, "I never thought I could be tempted to do that." This, of course, is folly. As long as we are in the flesh, we can be tempted.

Where Do I Get Power?

Two of Satan's most effective traps are the lure of knowledge and power. In a sense, everything is a matter of knowledge or, more accurately, truth, even the truth about power. Yet the power issue is so prominent in the experience of people around the world, we treat it as a separate issue.

Satan is a powerful angel. For whatever reason, God did not withdraw the power delegated to him as an angel when he rebelled against God and attempted to establish his own kingdom. We can be sure that his power is limited. God is the source of all power, and he delegates that power as he sees fit. Satan tries to create the impression that he is as powerful as or even more powerful than God, and Hollywood often conveys the same lie. For instance, the poor priest in *The Exorcist* was no match for Satan. People who have been involved in Satan-worship bear witness to this deception among the followers of Satan.

Satan is like an animal on a tether. The animal can go as far as the tether allows, but no farther. He can act freely within the area defined by his rope, but the rope defines his area of activity. Satan is on God's tether, and while he can do many things within the limited area defined by God, he certainly cannot go beyond the limits God has established. If he could, he would have reduced God's creation to chaos long ago. He is not happy that "the heavens declare the glory of God" (Ps 19:1) and that God's children can live to the glory of God.

Because his power is limited, however, does not mean that Satan has no power at all. He is able to do supernatural things. God gave him permission to incite an enemy against Job, send storms to destroy his property, and cause Job to suffer physically, but he was not allowed to take his life (see Job 1–2). He could give the Gadarene demonic strength to break every chain with which people tried to restrain him, but he could not resist Jesus' authority (see Mk 5:1-13). He could hinder Paul from carrying out some ministry he had planned, but he could not prevent the church from being planted (see 1 Thes 2:18).

It is also true, however, that if God's people trust and obey God, they can live free from the control that Satan would try to gain over them. The covenant God made with his people in the Old Testament can be stated quite simply: If you trust and obey me, I will give you the Promised Land, with all its blessings, and I will give you victory over all the attacks of your enemies. If you do not trust and obey me, I will allow your enemies to conquer you and deprive you of the blessings of the land.

God told Israel through Moses,

> This day I call heaven and earth as witnesses against you that
> I have set before you life and death, blessings and curses.
> Now choose life, so that you and your children may live and
> that you may love the Lord your God, listen to his voice, and
> hold fast to him. For the Lord is your life, and he will give
> you many years in the land he swore to give to your fathers,
> Abraham, Isaac, and Jacob.
>
> DEUTERONOMY 30:19-20

Notice the comparison: life and death, blessings and curses. We
like to talk about the blessings and we tend to expect them all
the time. We certainly don't like to think about the curses. In
this context the curse is simply God withdrawing his protection
and allowing the enemy to attack us. In the Old Testament it
was a military enemy. Today it is a spiritual enemy. The principle
is the same. Some people teach that God's protection for his
children is automatic; if you are a Christian, Satan can't do anything to you. That is not what the Scriptures teach. There are
some things Satan cannot do. He can't drive God out of our
lives. He cannot cause us to sin. He cannot tempt us beyond
what we are able to bear (see 1 Cor 10:13). He cannot pene-
trate the shield of faith, if we know the truth and choose to
believe it. But if we are not acting on the basis of faith and if we
are not following God's clear directions, Satan is able to gain a
foothold in our lives.

The new covenant of grace is written on our hearts rather
than on tablets of stone, and we enter into this covenant by
faith. If, however, we do not trust and obey, we forfeit God's

blessings. Jesus told the disciples in the Upper Room, "If you love me, you will obey what I command.... Whoever has my commands and obeys them, he is the one who loves me. He who loves me will be loved by my Father, and I too will love him and show myself to him" (Jn 14:15, 21). Lack of faith and obedience may not affect our salvation, but it does affect how we relate to our heavenly Father. Satan cannot rob us of our standing as children of God, but he can keep that relationship from being what God wants it to be, and he will do whatever he can to accomplish this.

One of those things is to tempt us with wrong sources of knowledge and power. Turning to occult practices for power and knowledge is saying, "I do not believe that God is faithful to his promise to supply all my needs. I do not believe that he has given us 'incomparably great power' (see Eph 1:19). That is why I need to try these other things." It shouldn't take any special discernment to recognize that such thinking comes from the pit, not from a loving Father. But Satan is a deceiver—not just a liar, but a very clever liar—and he has succeeded in seducing God's people in every age with his offers of power and knowledge to deal with the circumstances of life.

There is no reason to suppose that this has changed since biblical times. Satan is still in the business of using his deceptive power in any way he can. He does this in two entirely different ways. The first is to cause people to fear him. He wants to be feared because he wants to be worshipped. If we fear Satan more than we fear God, we elevate his limited attributes above the unlimited attributes of God.

He also wants to intimidate us with his power. Because he is a supernatural, spiritual being, Satan can cause those of us who are confined to the time-space world of planet Earth to be fearful of him and what he says he can do. He has the ability to appear in very threatening forms and to intimidate with visions of objects that create fear. Fallen angels do not have physical bodies and cannot assume bodies, but they can appear in a form visible to humans. While the Scriptures do not speak of this directly, it is generally assumed that this was what happened when Satan tempted Jesus in the wilderness. In any case, it is certainly true that many people have seen demonic figures in a wide variety of situations. The demon does not actually have a physical body, but he does appear that way.

Demons especially like to use this tactic with children. Children are very impressionable and can be frightened rather easily, especially at night. When children report seeing "things" in their rooms, parents often look around and report that there is nothing or no one there. They don't consider the possibility that the child really is seeing something in his or her mind with a spiritual vision that doesn't depend on the physical organs of sight. See my (Neil's) book *Spiritual Protection for Your Children* for a further discussion of this topic.[2]

The Lure of the Occult

Satan does not always appear as a fearsome, evil being. In fact, he rather seldom wears his Satan suit. If he showed up in red tights and horns, with a trident in his hand, we would recognize him in an instant. In dealing with Christians especially, he much prefers the "minister of righteousness" disguise. He comes as a friend who wants to help us.

He knows that a sense of significance is a basic need for us humans. If we are not finding that in our relationship with God, we will seek it elsewhere. An element in that feeling of significance is a sense of power—power to be someone significant, to do significant things. To feel that one has nothing that anybody wants or needs, that one is the low person on the totem pole, that one is not lovable, is the worst thing that can happen to a person.

Satan knows that, so he fosters that kind of thinking, and that kind of thinking sets us up for what are almost certain to be one of his next two temptations. He will suggest either self-destruction as an escape from the problem or taking power from the wrong source to try to solve the problem. Jesus made it clear that Satan came to steal, kill, and destroy (see Jn 10:10), so it is not surprising that Satan would suggest to people he attacks that they kill themselves. Suicide is a growing problem in the world. A surprising number of teenagers confess that they have had more than passing thoughts of taking their own lives.[3] It is the third leading cause of death among young people aged fifteen to twenty-four. It is the eighth leading cause of death among people of all ages in our country.

Sometimes, however, Satan will suggest that he can give us the power we need to meet the circumstances of our lives. Remember, he isn't wearing his Satan suit now. He is posing as a source of helpful information as to where power is available to help deal with life's problems. This opens a person to the whole world of the occult. The world of the occult says that there is a supernatural source of power and knowledge other than God—a source that is readily available to anyone who chooses to use it.

We have already said that Satan really does have some power that he can use in ways allowed by God. The problem is that he is not really interested in helping us with our need for power and significance. He will deliver only enough power or information to keep us coming back for more, but the price of taking from that source will be bondage in some other area of our lives. Some people question how anything that appears to be good could come from the devil. The answer is that he charges very high prices. He just doesn't tell us up front what the price will be. He is the master con artist. He has had many years of experience, and he knows us better than we know ourselves. He knows the area in our lives where we can most easily be tempted. For some people, this need for power is so great that they are rather easy marks for the offers of power from occult sources.

Another aspect to the lure of the occult is that it specializes in techniques. It says that if you know the right things to do, the right words to say, the right formulas to apply, you can get the power or knowledge you are seeking. We are drawn to the how-to-do-it approach. Our bookstores are filled with how-to-do-it books on all kinds of subjects. When it comes to dealing with problems around the house, those books can be very helpful; but when it comes to dealing with human problems, they can be very misleading if they do not lead us back to a relationship with the Creator. We can rest assured that finding the spiritual power we need for life is much more than a matter of technique, and we need to resist the lure of counterfeit knowledge and power.

God's View of the Occult

God has left us no room for doubt about his view of occult practices. He told his people as they were about to enter the Promised Land:

> When you enter the land the Lord your God is giving you, do not learn to imitate the detestable ways of the nations there. Let no one be found among you who sacrifices his son or daughter in the fire, who practices divination or sorcery, interprets omens, engages in witchcraft, or casts spells, or who is a medium or spiritist or who consults the dead. Anyone who does these things is detestable to the Lord, and because of these detestable practices the Lord your God will drive out those nations before you. You must be blameless before the Lord your God.
>
> DEUTERONOMY 18:9-13

If such practices were detestable to the Lord then, we can be sure they still are today, and all of them are still being practiced today—fortune-telling, witchcraft, séances, spiritism, even child sacrifice. God said that it was because of the commitment to and practice of these detestable things by the people living in Canaan that he was allowing Israel to drive them out.

Unfortunately, Israel did not heed the warning given to them by God, and they soon began to participate in the evil practices of the people in Canaan. When they did, God withdrew his hand of protection from them and allowed their enemies to defeat them. This is why both Israel and Judah were taken into captivity by pagan nations. It should not be surprising, then, that we find ourselves in some kind of bondage when we engage in practices which have always been condemned by the God we profess to love and obey.

A Winnable Battle

Yes, we are in a spiritual battle, and it is folly to think otherwise; but this is certainly not to suggest that we are helpless victims in the battle. We have all the resources necessary to win, but we have to use those resources. We are never promised automatic protection just because we are Christians, and the way to victory is not by using the right techniques. Israel had to do things God's way in order to win against their enemies, and that principle has not changed. We are free to live as God intends for us to live only when we live according to the truth. So, we turn next to a closer look at the role of truth in our relationship with God and with our enemy.

FIVE

Who Am I, Really?

What difference does it make what you think about yourself? Maybe a more accurate question is, what standards do you use to determine who you are? Or, even more accurately, *who* has a right to tell you who you are? How do you know what to believe about yourself?

How we answer these questions will determine how we will live, because we may not live what we profess, but we will always live what we believe. Or, to put it another way, we cannot behave consistently in a manner inconsistent with what we believe about ourselves. It should be clear by now that we believe that God is the only source of truth, and this includes the truth about who we are. We need to agree with God about ourselves, as well as about everything else in life.

Should I Love Myself?

In recent years a great many books and articles have been written on subjects like self-acceptance, self-image, self-confidence, and self-concept. Some authors argue strongly for the need to develop a healthy self-image. Others argue that any focus on the self is unbiblical. Jesus told us to deny ourselves. Some say that the commandment to "love your neighbor as yourself" (Mt 22:39) implies that we have to love ourselves first before we can love others as we love ourselves. What is the truth about loving or not loving ourselves?

As we noted with the words *world* and *flesh*, the word *self* is used in several very different ways. We thus need to ask which self we are talking about loving. It should be noted that there is no Greek word used in the New Testament that has a one-for-one correspondence with our English word *self*. Its use in the English translations is what we have to deal with, however, because we use it with several different meanings.

For example, in the instructions for observing the Day of Atonement, it was decreed that "anyone who does not deny himself on that day must be cut off from his people" (Lv 23:29). The meaning of denying oneself in this context is that the people of Israel were not to do their usual work on that day, in a manner consistent with Sabbath observance. It was not that the things they were to abstain from were bad. It was rather that the Day of Atonement was a very special day in the calendar of Israel, on which ordinary pursuits were to be set aside so that the focus could be on God and on his plan for dealing with the sins of his people.

We sometimes use the term *self-denial* in this way today. We deny ourselves legitimate things in order to pursue higher things. But this is not the denial of self that Jesus was talking about in his very forthright statement, "If anyone would come after me, *he must deny himself* and take up his cross and follow me" (Mk 8:34, emphasis added). The use of the term *self* in this implied command is with the meaning he had in mind when he said to the religious leaders of his day, "Woe to you, teachers of the law and Pharisees, you hypocrites! You clean the outside of

the cup and dish, but inside they are full of greed and *self*-indul-
gence" (Mt 23:25, emphasis added).

In Romans 2:8 Paul speaks of "those who are self-seeking
and who reject the truth and follow evil." This is the self that is
to be denied, or, as Paul puts it in Ephesians and Colossians, the
self that is to be "put off" (Eph 4:22; Col 3:9). It is being self-
centered rather than God-centered. It is evaluating ourselves
using our own criteria rather than saying about ourselves what
God says. It is attempting to be self-sufficient instead of finding
our sufficiency in Christ. Paul wrote, "Not that we are adequate
in ourselves to consider anything as coming from ourselves, but
our adequacy is from God" (2 Cor 3:5, NASB).

But there are two other uses of *self* that are very different
from either of the first two and have positive rather than negative connotations. One refers simply to the self that I am as a
person—the combination of physical and personality features
that make me who I am. Many people say in one way or another
that they believe God didn't do a very good job when he made
them. They would have chosen a very different combination of
traits—different height, different facial features, different talents, and on and on. That is like the pot telling the potter how
to do his work. The person God made each of us is not to be
denied or rejected but to be accepted as God's handiwork and
therefore loved.

The second positive use of *self* is what Paul means when he
says we are to "put on the new self, created to be like God in
true righteousness and holiness" (Eph 4:24). It is the new person each of us becomes by the grace of God. Paul told the
Corinthians, "If anyone is in Christ, he is a new creation" (2 Cor
5:17). This new creation is the Christ-centered and Spirit-filled
child of God who exhibits *self*-control (see Gal 5:23). This is the

meaning Jesus had in mind when he asked the people of his day, "What good is it for a man to gain the whole world, and yet lose or forfeit his very self?" (Lk 9:25). This new creation is to be affirmed, not denied. We need to agree with God's perception of who we are. It is the self in these last two senses that is to be loved.

The minute we say *love,* however, we have the same old problem of words meaning different things. The Greek had at least four separate words for different kinds of love. Three of the types of love depend upon one's emotional response to the loved object or person. *Eros* is the Greek word for sensual or erotic love. It is usually self-gratifying. *Storge* is parental love—another limited type of love. Mothers and parents in general have a love for their own offspring that is not shared to any extent outside the family. Even *philia,* friendship or brotherly love, is limited to those with whom one shares common interests, goals, or relationships. These three types of love are found in every culture.

Agape is another kind of love, however. The Greeks didn't speak of this type very often, because they thought it was essentially a quality of certain gods and was not a human quality. Essentially they were right, because "God is love" (1 Jn 4:16). God loves us because it is his nature to love us. That is why the love of God is unconditional. God's love is not dependent upon the object to be loved, but upon the nature of the lover. Since we have become partakers of his divine nature (see 2 Pt 1:4), we can be like Christ and love others because of who we are, not because of who they are or what they can do for us. Jesus contrasts his love with human love in Luke 6:32: "If you love those who love you, what credit is that to you? Even 'sinners' love those who love them."

It is this last kind of love to which we are referring when we speak of loving ourselves. It is not self-centeredness. It is not asking, "What do I think about myself?" or "What can I do for myself?" It is asking, "What does God say about me based on what he has already done for me?" then saying "I choose to agree with God." So, I thank God that he made me the way he did, including my body, my mind, and my talents; and I affirm his good purposes for me.

So, are we supposed to love ourselves? The answer is both yes and no. It depends on what you mean by self and what you mean by love.

God's Relationship to the Believer

If what God says about us is to be the basis of our belief about and attitude toward ourselves, we need to be sure that we know what God says. We can be sure that Satan does not want us to know and believe the truth, because he knows that our ability to live to the glory of God depends on our appropriation of God's gracious and good work in making and redeeming us. The battle for the mind begins right here in the life of a believer.

With this as background, let's look at figure 6 as it represents the relationship of the believer to God. There are two lines between them. One goes through the angels (the holy ones—that is, those angels who did not follow Satan in his rebellion). Notice that there is an arrow only at the bottom of the line, to indicate that this is a one-way connection. We at no time approach God through angels. They are God's "ministering spirits sent to serve those who will inherit salvation" (Heb 1:14). They serve God by carrying out his orders, but they are in no sense mediators between God and us.

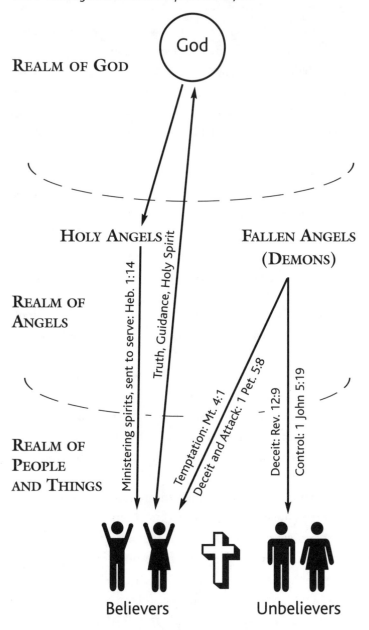

Figure 6: Believer's Relationship to God

The other line has arrows at both ends, indicating that this is a two-way relationship. God talks to us; we talk to God. We have fellowship with him (see 1 Jn 1:3). We have a love relationship with him (see Mt 22:37; Jn 15:9).

There are, of course, many things that could be said about this relationship, but let us establish two basic ideas as a foundation for what follows. First, our relationship with God must be based on the instruction, guidance, and empowerment of the Holy Spirit, and second, it must be based on truth. These ideas may seem so obvious that they hardly need to be mentioned to anyone who is a true believer. Experience teaches, however, that we are in trouble on both counts.

When it comes to the person and work of the Holy Spirit, we have no shortage of teaching on the subject. Theological works are readily available. The problem is that the books are too often written by theologians for other theologians, or at least for theological students, and not for the person in the pew. The problem is complicated because our worldview has conditioned us to believe that spirits don't really have much to do with what happens in our daily lives. We assume that we should do things much more on the basis of reason and scientific knowledge than on the basis of spiritual relationships. Spirits just aren't very real to most of us.

If you don't believe this, just imagine that you are having a discussion at home and that the discussion begins to be a little heated. Emotions begin to rise and bring the discussion to the level of an argument. What motivates you more to control those emotions: an important person showing up at the door (maybe the minister from your church) or the Holy Spirit there with you? "But," you say, "that's not fair. You can see a person, but you can't see the Holy Spirit."

True, but that is just the point. Paul tells us that "what is seen is temporary, but what is unseen is eternal" (2 Cor 4:18). What is the controlling factor—the temporary or the eternal? Our culture has affected us to a greater extent than we would like to believe. It has conditioned us to regulate our lives more on the basis of which other people are present than on which spirits are present, and to think more in terms of "common sense" or reason than in terms of revealed truth. The test of what we really believe is our actions, not what we say we believe. We all know better than we do, but in the area of spiritual activity, the gap is often much larger than we like to recognize. Our culture has squeezed us into its mold (see Rom 12:2, PHILLIPS) more than we acknowledge. This is another way of saying we are more worldly than we like to admit. Worldliness can be defined as conforming more to the expectations of our culture than to the expectations of God.

We have already said, however, that truth is life-changing when it is Spirit-taught. The reason there is often such a gap between what we know and what we do is that the Holy Spirit is not allowed to operate freely in our lives. We "grieve the Holy Spirit" (Eph 4:30) by actions and words that are clearly contrary to the fruit of love that is the hallmark of his presence in us (see Gal 5:22). First Corinthians 13 is a good measure of our spiritual maturity. Too often, however, the truth of the love chapter is in our minds but has not reached the level of Spirit-taught truth—the kind of truth that changes how we see ourselves and the way we behave.

This lack of reality in our relationship with the Holy Spirit is also the reason we may feel powerless against our enemy. It is the Spirit who empowers us to know the truth in the first place and then to live out the truth in our daily walk. It is Spirit-taught truth that sets us free and enables us to resist the deceptions of our enemy.

The relative unreality of the spirit world to most of us in the West applies not only to angels and the Holy Spirit. It carries over to the evil supernatural world as well. We may have a theological knowledge about Satan and demons, but that knowledge does not often lead to a functional faith in our relating to them. Our culture has adopted the idea of *demonizing* people and things, but the term has been reduced to a figure of speech, not a reference to reality. "Demons" are dealt with through the administration of powerful drugs and large doses of reason, not through the power of the Holy Spirit.

Admittedly, we can go too far in seeing demons behind human problems and can ascribe to them more power and influence than they possess.[1] Yet we can also go to the other extreme and not see them anywhere or any time. We (the authors) are not speaking against the proper use of medications or reason, but we are warning against trying to ignore in our daily living the role of evil spirits—the principalities and powers against which Paul says we "struggle" (Eph 6:12). The warnings of the New Testament about this enemy need to be taken seriously.

We have already noted that we have the capacity to hold truth intellectually without allowing that truth to actually guide the way we live. We can fill our brains with information—even true information—but it may lead to pride (see 1 Cor 8:1) or to profession of faith without corresponding life change (see Is 29:13; Mt 7:20; 23:27; Jas 2:18). Truth that does not transform is truth that is not believed. It is the idea behind the adage, "What you do hollers so loud I can't hear what you say."

This is a God-created and a God-sustained world. If we do

things God's way in God's world, God will be responsible for the results. If we do things our way in God's world, we have to be responsible for the results. Too many times we do things our way and then want to blame God for the results. It doesn't work that way. If we do not act on the basis of what God has defined as truth, we will not get the product that God planned when he gave us the truth.

Too often we practice what someone has called "selective obedience." That is to say, we have our list of spiritual truths that are in our comfort zone, and we readily obey those things. But there are other things that are outside our comfort zone, and we choose to act as if those things don't exist or at least don't apply to us.

Our emotional responses to each other too often are in the latter category. We, the authors, have had to learn that in our own marriages, and saying the truth about such things can be little short of revolutionary in relationships like marriage. You can sense when the other person is asking truth questions about some potentially tension-producing situation. The truth really does set us free (see Jn 8:32), not only from the penalty of sin, but also from the consequences of wrong emotions.

This opens a number of subjects that we cannot pursue at this point, but the issue is clear: we need to have a commitment to truth—to saying about everything in our lives what God says about it. You can be sure that Satan will take every opportunity to encourage wrong responses to things that trouble us. He, in fact, is a master at suggesting a wrong response. This is all part of spiritual warfare.

The sticky areas will vary from person to person. For some it is stewardship of money. For some it is stewardship of the body. For others, it is honesty. On and on the list could go.

Since Satan's primary tactic is deception, truth is an indispensable resource in resisting his attacks. The commitment to truth begins with the biblical and theological truth as revealed to us in the Scriptures. The revealed Word of God is the final authority for us in every area of life where the Word speaks. But there is another aspect of truth that is also critically important. That is plain honesty. We have to say the truth about what is going on in our lives.

Unfortunately, we, as a society, have become masters at not doing this. We have learned to play a game in church, a game that has just one rule: you don't make me take off my mask and I won't make you take off yours. If you grow up in a church group whose members are experts at mask-wearing, you learn to do it pretty well yourself before realizing how counterproductive it is.

The church ought to be a place where it is safe to be honest— a place where you can go to find help with the things that are really troubling you. All too often this is not true. Instead of finding safety and help in the church, we find other hurting people who don't know what to do with our hurts except talk about them to others, avoid us, or just try to act as if there were no problem.

It works like this. After moving to a new community my wife and I (Tim) went to a local church for the first time. We were greeted in the lobby by a warm, friendly person who introduced us to a few people, helped us find a good Sunday school class, and even invited us over for dinner. He was a preacher's dream. We learned later that he was a very gifted person who was a contributor to many different church and community activities.

After we had been in the church for a while, this person attended a class I was teaching on how to find freedom in

Christ. In that class we saw him take off his mask for the first time, and behind it was a bitter, angry person. It was not a pretty sight. Long-term relationships were documented in accusatory correspondence, and the man was eaten up by his bitterness. This had been going on for years. People close to him knew this, but in the church the reality had been carefully covered up. I am glad to report that we were able to help this person deal with his bitterness and come to a place where he could say, "I'm free! I'm free! I'm free!"

God will meet us only at the point of our honesty. He will not play the mask game with us. He will recognize our masks, but he will also say, "When you are ready to take off the mask and be honest about what is going on inside, I will be there to help you deal with it; but I cannot really help you until you take off the mask." You cannot be right with God and not be real. If necessary, God may have to make you real in order to be right with him.

As the deceiver, Satan encourages mask-wearing. He is the master of camouflage. He wears his own mask most of the time. He is expert at appearing as an "angel of light" or a "minister of righteousness" (see 2 Cor 11:13-15), and he encourages this behavior in those he is trying to influence. His purposes for us are served well by Christians who make a loud profession with the mask they wear while saying something quite different with the unchristian way they handle some areas of their lives.

The technical term for this behavior is hypocrisy, and the Christian alternative to it is sincerity. Hypocrisy is based on the idea of actors playing a part on the stage that is quite different from who they are in real life. To do this they sometimes use wax to create a new facial appearance. Our modern make-up artists in the entertainment industry have become real professionals at this.

Sincerity, on the other hand, in the original language meant "without wax," without a mask. Sincere persons are just who they are. What you see is what you get. They are honest to the point of transparency, rather than seeking to hide the truth or even to deny what they know to be true. They have come to know the "truth in the inner parts," which, according to David, is what God desires (see Ps 51:6).

David had to learn this lesson the hard way. Psalm 32 is a commentary on David's experience with sin. When he tried to cover up his sin, it even affected his physical body (v. 3). When he confessed, however—that is, when he said about his sin what God said about it—then he found forgiveness (v. 5) and could sing "songs of deliverance" (v. 7).

Sometimes our dishonesty is not an act of sin on our part, but a facet of our handling of abuse we have suffered. In this case we need to acknowledge that the abuse we have suffered does not mean that we are bad but that the abuse was wrong. Some people try to deal with their hurt by denying that it hurts. God can begin the healing process only when the hurt is acknowledged and the offender is forgiven. "Blessed are those who mourn, for they will be comforted" (Mt 5:4).

In being honest we often need to share our hurt and our sin with others. God put us in the body of Christ so that the body could provide its strength to us to help in the healing process, just as the healthy part of our physical bodies provides strength for a hurting part of the body. The church was intended by God to be a place where it is safe to be honest—a place where you can go to find help with the things that are really troubling you.

It is not too unusual to hear people say, "There is no one to whom I can talk." What they mean is that there is no one they trust to handle the truth about them with love and with the hope of finding resolution to their problem. What is more surprising is to hear someone who has been in counseling—even Christian counseling—say, "I have never told this to anyone before, but ..." People can manipulate counselors by what they don't tell them, and they probably do not tell them everything because they are still not sure that the person trying to help them really cares or *can* help them find resolution for their problems. The adage is, "People don't care how much you know until they know how much you care," and mature Christians ought to be the ones who help others know how much God cares by the care we show to them. What we usually call counseling is often discipling—learning the truth about God and the truth about our relationship to him. If young Christians were properly discipled, many of the problems that later take them to professional counselors would not develop.

Living free in Christ begins with a commitment to truth—the truth about God, and the truth about what God says concerning us.

Who Am I?

We began by asking the question, who are we, really? We haven't fully answered that question, but we can say that Satan wants to give us all the wrong answers to the question and that God is the source of truth in seeking the right answer. We must always begin by speaking the truth about our sin, but we need to go on from there to speak the truth about who we are as

God's redeemed children. In order to speak the truth about anything, including what it means to be God's child, we need to be sure that we are seeking to relate to God for who he really is. We thus turn next to a fuller look at that subject.

SIX

Which God Do I Serve?

The battle for the mind begins with a true belief in God. How we perceive him will determine how we perceive almost everything else in life and how we relate to life itself. Satan knows this, and that is why he almost always begins his attacks on us by trying to give us a twisted view of God. This is critically important, because while we may not practice what we profess, we will always practice what we really believe. For this reason, we need to examine our basic belief system, and this belief system always begins with how we view God.

The Serpent Is Still at It

We have already noted how the serpent tempted Eve in the Garden of Eden. Let's go back to that scene and make some further observations about that encounter. The serpent (Satan) first deceived Eve into questioning whether God and his Word could really be trusted. He said, "Has God said that you will die if you eat of that tree? That's not true. You won't die. You will become like God himself, knowing good and evil. You won't have to take your orders from him any more because your judgment is as good or even better than his. You will be better off if you do what you think is right than if you do what he says. You see, God just cannot be trusted completely" (Gn 3:1,4-5, author's paraphrase).

There was also the implication that God did not really love them, or he wouldn't have withheld this wonderful fruit from them. The Scriptures tell us that the fruit was "good for food and pleasing to the eye, and also desirable for gaining wisdom" (Gn 3:6). How could God really love them and withhold this wonderful "blessing" from them? It is clear that Satan was seeking to undermine the character of God, and once Adam and Eve began to doubt God's trustworthiness and his love, it was not difficult for the serpent to lead them to break the one negative command God had given them.

The irony of all this is that it is like a child standing beside an overflowing toy box, saying, "I don't have anything to do. You won't let me play with the matches." Why do children so often seem to focus on the one thing they know they shouldn't have? Even for adults, the forbidden fruit seems to be the most desirable. God had told Adam and Eve that they could eat from all of the other trees in the garden. It wasn't like they didn't have wonderful fruit on many other trees. All they had to do to remain in perfect fellowship with their Creator was to obey one command. They couldn't have had it much easier. Yet, when they doubted whether God could be trusted, they now had to make all of their own decisions. If God couldn't be trusted in one thing, he couldn't be trusted in any. If their judgment was better than God's in this matter, it might be better than God's in every other matter. That kind of responsibility was overwhelming.

Satan is a clever deceiver—an experienced con man. What appeared on the surface to be only a matter of eating or not eat-

ing fruit from one tree had much more far-reaching consequences than they ever dreamed. Before this they had had an
open, trusting relationship with God. Now they found themselves hiding from him for reasons they didn't even understand.
They had lost the security of that relationship. Before, their
needs had all been met by what God had provided for them in
the garden and by their relationship with him. Now they had
lost their trusting relationship with him, and they were about to
lose the whole garden. Before they fell for Satan's lies, their
human need for significance had been met by their relationship
with their Creator. Now they had lost that relationship, and
with it their significance as his children.

Sin always has consequences that Satan never suggests when
he dangles the forbidden fruit in front of us. Even after the sin
has been confessed and forgiven, the consequences are still present. The angry words can never be taken back. The physical or
emotional injury caused to another person can never be
undone. The life that was destroyed can never be restored. And
it all begins when we see God as something or someone other
than who he really is.

Counterfeit Gods

Since his first success in the Garden of Eden, Satan has gone on
to bigger and bigger lies about God. He has convinced some
people that there is no such person as God (see Ps 53:1) and no
supernatural power. What you see in this world is all you get, he
says. There is no life beyond the grave.

Sometimes the counterfeit god that Satan suggests is the universe itself. Everything and every person is said to be part of

god. One simply cannot separate the spiritual and the physical, because they are all one. This belief is characteristic of many Asian religions and is the belief system behind many of the practices that come from that part of the world.

New Age teachers in the West have adopted this view of god and the world. They tell us our primary sin is in not recognizing that we are really god, or at least part of god, and that we can control our own destiny by exercising our godness. We do not need a Savior to die for our sins. There is psychic power in the universe that we can learn to manipulate in order to make it do what we want it to do. These teachers also include animistic ideas of spirits and power in their teachings. There is, however, nothing really new about the New Age. It is as old as biblical history. Its proponents have just changed the terms from *medium* to *channeler* and from *demons* to *spirit guides*.

A variation on this theme is a god who is not the world itself, but isn't really a person either. It is an impersonal world soul. This god is like an ocean, and people on earth are drops of water. The ideal is to join your drop of water to the ocean, so that it can never be an individual drop again. Millions believe that they are just some insignificant part of some cosmic unity which lacks any meaningful purpose.

Some add to their belief system all kinds of other gods which are personal but who share all the worst qualities of fallen human beings, like the gods in the Greek and Roman cultures of biblical times. We call this polytheism. These pantheons of gods might have one high god above the others, but the role of the God of the Bible as Creator, Sustainer, and Savior has been lost.

Some come closer to the truth by seeing their god as the creator of the world, but he is very far away and virtually impossible to reach. Others believe that he is a very powerful but also a very arbitrary kind of god, quite unapproachable by mere humans. Relating to him is reduced to recitation of a creed, an endless repetition of memorized prayers, and certain prescribed activities. This, however, does not meet a person's need for a relationship with God, so they also add all kinds of magic and sorcery to their religious life. We have already seen that such things are Satan's way of bringing people under his influence and ultimate control.

A Depersonalized Christian God

You may be saying, "Thank God, we are not like that. We Bible-believing Christians know who God really is." The problem is, as we have noted already, we may know truth intellectually, but that does not guarantee that we practice it in everyday life. We may, in fact, become practical atheists. We can know all about God yet not know him at all. We can profess to know God but live as though he doesn't exist.

A seminary professor courageously shared his own experience with this in a widely read Christian journal.[1] He said that he prided himself on his knowledge of the Scripture and on saying, "The Bible is enough." However, when his little boy was diagnosed with renal cell carcinoma, a virtually untreatable and incurable form of cancer, he said, "Quite frankly, I found that the Bible was not the answer. I found the Scriptures to be helpful—even authoritatively helpful—as a guide. But without my feeling God, the Bible gave me little solace." He went on to explain:

In the midst of this "summer from hell," I began to examine what had become of my faith. I found a longing to get closer to God, but found myself unable to do so through my normal means: exegesis, Scripture reading, more exegesis. I believe that I had depersonalized God so much that when I really needed him I didn't know how to relate. I longed for him, but found many community-wide restrictions in my [theological] environment. I found a suffocation of the Spirit in my evangelical tradition as well as in my own heart.[2]

Yes, even professors of the Bible can profess more about God than they live out in daily life. A god who is confined to the pages of theology books and even of the Bible is not the God who wants to use the knowledge gained from the books to lead us into a personal relationship with him—even into a love relationship with him. We can become like the Pharisees, to whom Jesus said, "You diligently study the Scriptures because you think that by them you possess eternal life. These are the Scriptures that testify about me, yet you refuse to come to me to have life" (Jn 5:39-40). Satan does not object to orthodox theology as long as it does not lead to an intimate knowledge of God.

Caricatures of God

Another way in which our enemy tries to corrupt our view of God is to sell us caricatures of God. Have you ever seen an artist doing caricatures in a mall or at a fair? We had one made of our son once, and it is kind of scary to see what distortions can be included in such pictures. Caricatures are often drawn of public figures like politicians. In a caricature one physical characteristic is exaggerated—like a big chin or nose, protruding ears, unusual hairdo, or pear-shaped body. You can usually tell who has been caricatured, but the drawing is not an accurate portrayal of that person.

Satan tries to do this with God. The Bible says God is our judge, so Satan emphasizes his role as judge out of all proportion to his role as loving father or shield and protector or giver of good gifts. Some people report that no matter what they read in the Bible, they feel condemned. God is always seen as a judge, condemning them for every conceivable way in which they come short of perfection.

For some, God is the opposite of this. He is the kindly old grandfather who sees his legitimate role as one who spoils his grandchildren. Far from correcting them when they do something wrong, he may laugh at their sins and say they are cute. Either extreme pleases Satan equally well.

God Seen Through a Filter

Our view of God often comes to us through one or more filters, which distort the proper image. Cameras are made to take accurate pictures of the subject being photographed, but the photographer can put a filter over the lens to deliberately enhance or distort the image recorded on the film. A bright, sunny day can be turned into a dull, cloudy day with the right filter. Day can be turned into night with the right filter. Colors can be changed with the right filter. Satan knows that our view of God often comes to us through other people, and he will use this as a means of distorting the true image of God in the impression made on our minds. Figure 7 suggests how this filtering process works.

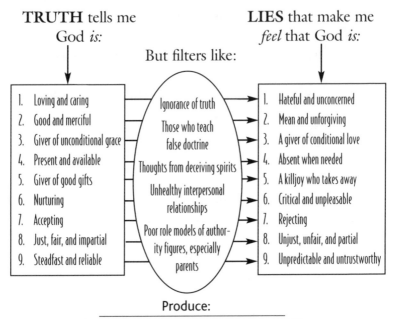

TRUTH tells me God *is:*

But filters like:

LIES that make me *feel* that God *is:*

1. Loving and caring		1. Hateful and unconcerned
2. Good and merciful	Ignorance of truth	2. Mean and unforgiving
3. Giver of unconditional grace	Those who teach false doctrine	3. A giver of conditional love
4. Present and available		4. Absent when needed
5. Giver of good gifts	Thoughts from deceiving spirits	5. A killjoy who takes away
6. Nurturing	Unhealthy interpersonal relationships	6. Critical and unpleasant
7. Accepting		7. Rejecting
8. Just, fair, and impartial	Poor role models of authority figures, especially parents	8. Unjust, unfair, and partial
9. Steadfast and reliable		9. Unpredictable and untrustworthy

Produce:

Figure 7: God Seen Through a Filter

Simple ignorance of the truth about God increases the possibility for taking one's knowledge from a wrong source. God said, concerning Israel in the time of Hosea, "My people are destroyed from lack of knowledge" (Hos 4:6), and this is true in any age. What we do not know can hurt us, especially when it is knowledge as crucial to our well-being as a correct view of God.

When we do not know the truth, we are subject to deception from false prophets and false teachers. Cults prey on Christians who have a desire to know God but who have not come into a personal relationship with him, or those who have heard and received the gospel message but have not been discipled well. Cults or cultlike expressions of the church offer these people a form of discipling, but it is dependent on following only a self-appointed leader and is based on a wrong view of God.

In chapter two we saw how Satan can put thoughts into our minds. This is what is behind Paul's statement to his "son in the faith," Timothy: "The Spirit clearly says that in later times some will abandon the faith and follow deceiving spirits and things taught by demons" (1 Tm 4:1). This teaching often comes through false teachers, as we have just noted, but it may also come through thoughts placed directly in the mind of a person by Satan or one of his fallen angels. This is one of the primary means of temptation in general, but in this case, it is a means of bringing a person into bondage through wrong and even blasphemous views of God. It is not unusual for people to report that they hear voices in their minds condemning them or suggesting blasphemous thoughts to them.

Satan will try to get you to believe that these are your own thoughts, and if you fall for this you will be in bondage to the lies you believe. The con artist is at work again. He uses this filter to skew our view of God. He knows how vulnerable we are to such deception. We need to know that our defense is to "take captive every thought to make it obedient to Christ" (2 Cor 10:5).

Dysfunctional relationships with other people, especially with authority figures, are often the filter that distorts our view of God. These relationships may be with teachers, pastors, coaches, employers, or anyone with whom we develop a close relationship. By far the most important persons in this category are parents. We very easily carry over our view of an earthly father to our heavenly Father. The parent for whom nothing we do is ever good enough may cause our view of God to come through the filter as a God who is impossible to please, whose demands always exceed our ability to meet them. A parent who is abusive may filter our view of God into one who finds more pleasure in punishing us than in blessing us.

We have all been victimized in some way, but whether we remain victims is really our choice. Nobody can fix our past, and even God doesn't try to do that. He makes us a new creation in Christ and sets us free from our past. We have to choose to believe the truth that will set us free. The true knowledge of God and who we are as his children is what liberates us.

Satan is clever enough to recognize that if he can get us to buy his wrong view of God, we will almost certainly have a wrong view of what it means to be a child of God. We will look at this more carefully in the next chapter, but first we need to look at one more common way in which our view of God becomes distorted.

The Hard-to-Please God

Have you seen yourself looking through any of these filters? Most people do, but perhaps you are feeling good about your view of God so far. There is one more very common error in our thinking about God.

Look at the following words:

Authority

Accountability

Affirmation

Acceptance

How do you sense God coming to you? Does he say, "As you are accountable to my authority, I will affirm and accept you?" Or does he say, "I accept you and affirm you and ask for accountability to my authority?" An evangelical pastor who came for help with a behavioral problem was asked this question, and with almost no hesitation he said, "Oh, it is from the top down. I have to conform to God's expectations of me if I expect him to affirm me." My answer to him was, "Do you know what you have just told me? You have said you believe that you have to earn the grace of God. I have to tell you that that is absolutely impossible. You can never get to acceptance and affirmation by God through the avenue of your behavior, because 'by observing the law no one will be justified' (Gal 2:16). That is true on the day you are saved and on every day after that."

When authority figures demand accountability without acceptance and affirmation, they will never get it. But when authority figures grant acceptance and affirmation, their subjects voluntarily become accountable.

One of Satan's favorite lies about God is that we have to be good enough to be loved and accepted by him, and that God is pretty hard to please. God's standards are very high, Satan will tell you, and when you think you are about there, you will discover that the goal has been moved out a little farther. Most Christians know in their minds that this is not true, but when we examine the way they live, their actions often deny their profession.

Our whole society is performance-based. You get what you earn. You earn your way up the corporate ladder, the social ladder, the academic ladder, the arts ladder, the sports ladder, and on and on. There is no free lunch—not even a free breakfast at the motel. The signs should read, "Breakfast included in the price of the room" rather than "Free breakfast."

When we bring that kind of thinking into our relationship with God, however, we have a major theological problem, because we are acceptable to God on one basis and one basis only—what God has done for us in Christ, not what we do for him. There are two wrong ways to look for acceptance. One is to continually take our own spiritual temperature to see if we are "good enough." When we do this, we will be trapped either in pride or in feelings of inferiority and inadequacy. Only God can give us a right view of ourselves and fulfill our need for affirmation and acceptance.

The other place we look for acceptance is from other people. Peer pressure tends to control our lives from infancy through old age. Children have to have the latest toys that all their friends have. As adults we have to keep up with the neighbors. We focus on our appearance and performance in order to be accepted by important people. We adopt behavioral patterns that are expected by the "in group" of which we want to be a part. We strive for mastery in some area of life in order to receive the praise of people. Even pastors can be caught in this trap. We all long for acceptance and affirmation. If our functional faith does not include a God who is unconditionally loving and abounding in grace—qualities that result in acceptance and affirmation—we turn to people for the acceptance and affirmation that we need.

Everyone needs to be loved. No human, however, is capable of giving unconditional love and acceptance. We have to begin with a God who loves because it is his nature to love (see 1 Jn 4:8). As humans we tend to love people who are lovable, and therefore we tend to expect God to love only what we consider lovable. The tendency to create God in our own image or in the image of significant others is one of the devil's favorite strategies for trapping us in his lies.

We also need to begin with a God who expresses his love in grace. In order to understand the grace of God, we need to review some definitions. The first term we need to understand is *justice*. Justice is getting what you deserve. A man accused of a crime stands before the judge, who says, "You're guilty. The penalty is death." We can be glad that God does not deal with us on the basis of justice.

Mercy means not getting what you deserve. The accused stands before the judge, who says, "You're guilty, but I am waiving the sentence. You are free." God cannot be unjust, so the penalty for sin had to be paid, and Jesus did that at the cross. "God made him who had no sin to be sin for us, so that in him we might become the righteousness of God" (2 Cor 5:21). Justice and mercy meet at the cross. Paul wrote to Titus, "When the kindness and love of God our Savior appeared, he saved us, not because of righteous things we had done, but because of his mercy" (Ti 3:4-5). God's mercy, which offers us forgiveness and freedom from the penalty for sin, is indeed great good news. Unfortunately, this is where most presentations of the gospel end.

There is more, however: There is *grace*. Grace is getting what you could never deserve. The accused stands before the judge, who says, "You're guilty, but I am waiving the sentence, and I am going to adopt you and make you my heir." Paul tells us that "the Spirit himself testifies with our spirit that we are God's children. Now if we are children, then we are heirs—heirs of God and co-heirs with Christ" (Rom 8:16-17).

Which God?

So, which God do you worship and serve? Is he one who has been distorted by the filters of the world and the enemy of our souls? Or is he the utterly trustworthy God whose Word is forever settled in heaven (see Ps 119:89)? Is he a hard-to-please God who keeps moving the standard just a little higher? Or is he the God who loves you with unconditional love—love that does not depend on how lovable you are, but on his very nature as love? Is he the God of the Bible? Or an idol of your own making? Is he a person you really know? Or is he a caricature—a cartoon figure—that you carry in your mind?

To win the spiritual battle for our minds, we must have a true view of God. That is why Paul prayed for the Ephesians "that the God of our Lord Jesus Christ, the Father of glory, may give to you a spirit of wisdom and of revelation in the knowledge of him" (Eph 1:17, NASB). This could be translated as "full knowledge" or "right knowledge." Paul always begins his letters with theology in general, but here he begins with the theology of God in particular. It is like Paul is saying, "I know Satan will be trying to pervert your view of God; so I want to begin by making sure that you know who God really is." This is where we all need to begin our spiritual pilgrimage.

SEVEN

Keep Looking Down

Down? Yes, down, from where we are seated with Christ in the heavenly realms (see Eph 2:6). This position, seated with Christ, is not just something that we will attain in the future. Being "in Christ" is a present reality for the true believer. Unfortunately, too many of us spend our time living "under the circumstances." The fact is, however, that we are never the helpless victims of our circumstances. We may very well be the victims of the way we *look* at our circumstances, but in Christ we can always be "more than conquerors." Let's look at this idea of how we should see ourselves "in Christ."[1]

Adopted Into His Family

The Scriptures use many figures of speech to help us understand our relationship to God. Among them are potter and the pot, branches and vine, shepherd and sheep, Lord and disciples, King and subjects, children by birth, and children by adoption.

The idea of adoption is used by Paul in Ephesians 1:4-5: "In love he predestined us to be adopted as his [children] through Jesus Christ in accordance with his pleasure and will." Adoptions don't happen by accident. The adoptive parents want the child, and they choose to act on their desires. So Paul tells us that God chose to adopt us as his children, "in accordance with his *pleasure* and *will*" (Eph 1:5, emphasis added).

Jesus said to the Pharisees, "You are of your father the devil" (Jn 8:44). The idea of being part of Satan's family by virtue of being born with the curse of Adam's sin on us is what is behind the idea of adoption. God does not adopt us out of our earthly families. Adoption into his family may, however, affect the way we relate to our earthly families. We no longer need to see ourselves as the victims of the way we were treated by our parents or families, because God has now made us part of his family—a family where the Father loves with unconditional love and can be depended upon to use his limitless power to carry out what his love chooses to do.

Who Tells Me Who I Am?

I (Tim) grew up in a church setting that told me in one way or another that you had to be almost perfect to be acceptable to God. We call this approach to defining our relationship to God legalism. That, coupled with the fact that I was part of a large family facing financial problems in the Great Depression years of the thirties, helped me develop a full-blown inferiority complex. I saw everyone as better than I was—especially socially and financially. I thought I could never be good enough for God to use me.

In the last chapter we saw how various circumstances can filter the image of God to us, resulting in a distorted image of him. The same filters work with our view of ourselves, as indicated in Figure 8.

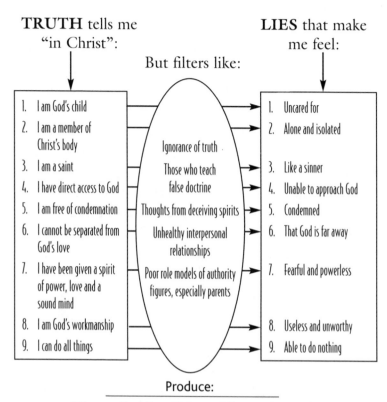

TRUTH tells me "in Christ":

1. I am God's child
2. I am a member of Christ's body
3. I am a saint
4. I have direct access to God
5. I am free of condemnation
6. I cannot be separated from God's love
7. I have been given a spirit of power, love and a sound mind
8. I am God's workmanship
9. I can do all things

But filters like:

Ignorance of truth

Those who teach false doctrine

Thoughts from deceiving spirits

Unhealthy interpersonal relationships

Poor role models of authority figures, especially parents

LIES that make me feel:

1. Uncared for
2. Alone and isolated
3. Like a sinner
4. Unable to approach God
5. Condemned
6. That God is far away
7. Fearful and powerless
8. Useless and unworthy
9. Able to do nothing

Produce:

Figure 8: Myself Seen Through a Filter

The list of who I am "in Christ" could be much longer. But let's look at this from another perspective. We noted in the last chapter that we live in a very performance-based society. Our status in society is often based on what we do and say, whether good or bad. We constantly compare ourselves with other people, and we are deeply concerned about what people think of us. Our behavior is very often determined by what other people say we are or by what we think they say we are, rather than by who we perceive ourselves to be "in Christ." This is peer pressure at work again.

Since we were all born dead in our trespasses and sins (see Eph 2:1), we had neither the presence of God in our lives nor the knowledge of his ways. Therefore we have had to make a name for ourselves and earn a sense of worth according to the world system in which we have been raised. The primary basis for this pursuit is our appearance, performance, and status. Such attempts at self-verification, however, always crumble under hostile criticism or morbid introspection.

At the same time, we all do things that are not affirmed by others. In fact, some of our best efforts are condemned by others. This may be due to just plain sin, but it may also be due to a simple mistake or even a lack of affirmation for genuine achievement.

An example of the latter is the boy who got C's on his report card. His father told him that if he worked hard, he could get B's. The boy worked hard and got some B's, but when he presented his report to his father, the father said, "Well, if you really worked hard, you could get A's." The boy really worked hard and brought home some A's, expecting that he would finally get some affirmation from his father. The father viewed the card and said, "You probably have an easy teacher."

It is reported that children in this country get seven to ten shame messages for every affirming message they receive, yet it takes many affirming messages to offset the effect of one shame message. If it isn't people who provide the shame messages, it is Satan and his corps of demons. Satan is called the "accuser of our brothers" (Rv 12:10), and he loves to accuse us of anything he can. It seems like we each have a little imp sitting on our shoulders, telling us how bad we are. Satan knows that if we have a negative perception of ourselves, we will behave in essentially negative ways. From there on, it doesn't matter what new truth we learn. Unless we apply the truth about our identity "in Christ," no amount of behavior modification is going to turn us into Spirit-led Christians. "A person cannot consistently behave in a way that's inconsistent with how he perceives himself."[2]

Experience tells us that many, if not most, Christians swing back and forth between trying hard and giving up—trying hard to do and say the things that will bring affirmation, but getting enough shame messages that they feel like giving up.

Agreeing With God About Who We Are

We spoke earlier about loving ourselves and defining that as saying about ourselves what God says about us. Let's look at this in terms of the adoption figure with which we began this chapter.

Adoption is very meaningful to me (Tim) because I have two children by adoption. My wife and I both lost our first mates through seemingly untimely deaths, and when God led us together, she brought two small children from her first marriage. In adopting the children, I had to appear before a judge, who looked me in the eye and said, "Sir, do you understand that in adopting these children, you must make them equally your heirs with any children that will be born to your marriage?"

I quickly replied, "Your Honor, I understand that, and I gladly accept it." My wife and I have had two children by our marriage, so I have four children, but I never think of the children as different. They are all my children, and if you were to read my will, you would find no mention of adoption or stepchildren. I have four equal heirs.

In Romans 8:16-17, Paul says, "The Spirit himself testifies with our spirit that we are God's children. Now if we are children, then we are heirs—heirs of God and co-heirs with Christ." Do you understand that? If you do, you are ahead of me. With the legalism and perfectionism in my background, and my inferiority feelings, it is difficult to think of myself as a prince in God's kingdom. "A prince or princess?" you ask. Yes, isn't that what a co-heir to the king would be? You are not being prideful when you believe this truth, but you are defeated if you don't.

Do you see why Satan doesn't want you to believe this? If you did, and you started to live like royalty in God's kingdom, you would bring glory to God in a way impossible when you are dragging your tail between your legs and saying you're no good. You may upgrade the "no good" to "just a sinner saved by grace." But as great as having our sins forgiven and being "saved" is, it is only half of the gospel. The other half is understanding and accepting the fact that God has "raised us up with Christ and seated us with him in the heavenly realms in Christ Jesus" (Eph 2:6). This is the grace gift we have already spoken of—the judge pardoning the accused and then adopting him into his own family and making him his heir.

Going back to the try hard-give up idea,[3] the problem with that picture is that this is not the way we should be defining our belief about who we are. Paul said, "When they measure themselves by themselves and compare themselves with themselves, they are not wise" (2 Cor 10:12). We should get our identity from an entirely new source, namely, who we are in Christ based on what God has already done for us, not what we have done, whether good or bad. Then we can rest rather than struggle, because victory ultimately depends on what God has already done, not on what we try to do.

There is an interesting and illuminating illustration of this in the life of the great missionary pioneer and founder of the China Inland Mission, J. Hudson Taylor. As a young man, Taylor had the vision to go into the interior of China, a place where in the 1850s no missionary had yet ventured. To prepare himself for this, he adopted a very disciplined lifestyle. He ate a very Spartan diet. He cut himself off from sources of money so he could learn to trust God to supply his needs. He was an amazing young man.

He went to China as he planned. He adopted Chinese dress and even let his hair grow so that he could wear it in a long braid in order to identify more fully with the people he was trying to reach with the gospel. He eventually founded a new mission and asked God for one hundred missionaries and enough money in big gifts to send them out so he wouldn't have a lot of bookkeeping. God answered his prayer! The record says, however, that when Taylor went around to visit the mission stations, there was a sense of tension between this super-spiritual, super-disciplined leader and the missionaries.

About midlife, Taylor's biography quotes him as saying, "Unbelief was, I felt, *the* damning sin of the world—yet I indulged in it."[4] Hudson Taylor, guilty of unbelief? How could that be? His faith seemed to put him on a pedestal so high an ordinary mortal could hardly touch him. What was he talking about?

In terms of our present discussion, he said, "I discovered that I was on the 'try hard' cycle of my own effort in order to impress God and myself and everyone else how committed I was to God. I discovered that he wanted me to rest in what he had done for me. I was simply not believing and receiving the gracious gift provided for me in Christ." After he learned this lesson, Taylor's favorite song became,

> Jesus, I am resting, resting, in the joy of what thou art.
> I am finding out the greatness of thy loving heart.
> Thou hast bid me gaze upon thee, and thy beauty fills my soul;
> For by thy transforming power, thou hast made me whole.[5]

History also reports that from that time on, when Taylor made his rounds to visit the missionaries, there was an overflow of blessing from his life, rather than a feeling of tension. When he exchanged his performance-based approach to Christianity for a grace-based relationship with his Savior, his behavior changed. Yes, people—even missionaries—may not live what they say they believe, but they will always live what they really believe.

Paul has an interesting commentary on this in Romans 5, and to put Paul's theology on the lower shelf for easier access, we quote from the Living Bible:

> So now, since we have been made right in God's sight by faith in his promises, we can have real peace with him *because of what Jesus Christ our Lord has done for us.* For because of our faith, he has brought us into this place of highest privilege where we now stand [seated with God in the heavenlies in Christ], and we confidently and joyfully look forward to

actually becoming all that God has had in mind for us to be [as his adopted children].

We can rejoice, too, when we run into problems and trials for we know that they are good for us—they help us learn to be patient. And patience develops strength of character in us and helps us trust God more each time we use it until finally our hope and faith are strong and steady. Then, when that happens, we are able to hold our heads high no matter what happens and know that all is well, for we know how dearly God loves us, and we feel this warm love everywhere within us because God has given us the Holy Spirit to fill our hearts with his love.

ROMANS 5:1-5, LB, emphasis added

Does holding our heads high no matter what happens sound like pride? It would be if it were based on the try hard cycle. But it isn't. It is based on what God has done for us in Christ. It is the result of receiving his gracious gift to us—adoption into his family. And, we repeat, not believing this is not humility, it is unbelief, in spite of what Satan may try to tell you to the contrary.

The feelings of inferiority that most of us have to deal with are the result of being self-centered—of asking what we think about ourselves. Humility is never self-centered; it is God-centered. It is confidence properly placed[6]—in God, not in ourselves. Inferiority feelings are Satan's counterfeit for true humility.

We need to recognize also, however, that the path to the "strong and steady" hope and faith leads through learning to deal with "problems and trials." Most of us would like to avoid that part of the journey, but as a good and wise Father, God wants us as his children to develop the "strength of character" that can come in no other way. How we handle the hard places in life will depend on whether we see ourselves as under the circumstances or far above them.

Figure 9 shows the believer seated "in Christ" in the heavenly realms. It is from this perspective that we look at ourselves and our circumstances. Things look very different from up there. Our prayers don't have to go above the ceiling. They just have to go to our Father, with whom we are sitting in a love relationship. The Bible is read with the author at our side. Witnessing becomes simply living out our position as joint heirs with Christ—a position which makes us spiritual princes and princesses in his kingdom. Resisting the devil also is very different from this perspective. If you see yourself as a victim, way down at the bottom of the chart, you will be very reluctant to stand against a powerful spiritual enemy so far above you. But seated with God in the heavenlies, with your hand on the arm of the throne of God, you can resist him "steadfastly in the faith" (1 Pt 5:9).

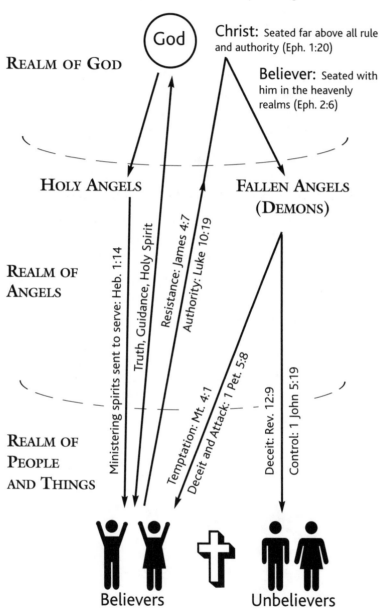

Figure 9: Warfare Relationships

So, Keep Looking Down!

Now do you understand why we say, "Keep looking down"? It all depends on where you are looking down from. Being "in Christ" changes your perspective on many things—prayer, witnessing, reading the Bible, resisting the enemy. It also changes your perspective on suffering. Paul says, "I consider that our present sufferings are not worth comparing with the glory that will be revealed in us" (Rom 8:18). Being a co-heir with Jesus means that there is glory waiting for us—the glory that Satan wanted and will never get, but which is now our sure inheritance as children of God. Few of us have suffered as much as Paul did, so we need to listen to him when he tries to help us see things from our position "in Christ."

EIGHT

Boot Camp for Reluctant Warriors

When recruits enter the armed forces they go first to boot camp if they are sailors or marines or to basic training if they are soldiers. That is where they are prepared physically and mentally for participation in war. Most participants hope there won't be a real war and they will not have to use the things they are learning (they're reluctant warriors), but preparedness is the name of the game. Other things being equal, a well-trained and well-equipped army is going to prevail over one that is poorly trained and not well equipped.

That principle readily transfers to participation in spiritual warfare. There can be no doubt that the enemies we are up against have had many years of experience in this kind of warfare. They have been coached well and have learned from experience what works and what doesn't.[1] To go into combat against this enemy without a good boot camp would be folly, yet that is what many are trying to do.

Your Spiritual Bulletproof Vest

When spiritual warfare is mentioned, the passage of Scripture which most readily comes to mind is Ephesians 6, where Paul says:

Finally, be strong in the Lord and in his mighty power. Put on the full armor of God so that you can take your stand against the devil's schemes. For our struggle is not against flesh and blood, but against the rulers, against the authorities, against the powers of this dark world and against the spiritual forces of evil in the heavenly realms. Therefore put on the full armor of God, so that when the day of evil comes, you may be able to stand your ground, and after you have done everything, to stand.

EPHESIANS 6:10-13

In this letter to the Ephesians, Paul has said many things about this warfare,[2] and now he reaches a climax in chapter 6 by being quite specific about the nature of our enemy and the things we need to do to stand against him successfully. The place to begin is to admit that we are in a battle and to recognize that that enemy is the devil and his host of fallen angels. We often get sidetracked fighting each other, but Paul makes it clear that the real battle is with Satan. The people of his day would understand the spiritual nature of the battle much more readily than we twenty-first-century Westerners do, but that does not change the reality of the struggle.

Next we need to make sure that we have a proper uniform to wear. One of the first things that happens in boot camp is the issuing of uniforms—articles of clothing that have been designed and field-tested with military life in view. This image of putting on spiritual clothing is interpreted by some New Testament writers as applying to the Christian life in general (see Rom 13:14; Gal 3:27; Eph 4:24; Col 3:10-14), but here Paul applies it to spiritual warfare in particular. He counsels us, as he did the Ephesians:

Therefore put on the full armor of God, so that when the day of evil comes, you may be able to stand your ground, and after you have done everything, to stand. Stand firm then, with the belt of truth buckled around your waist, with the breastplate of righteousness in place, and with your feet fitted with the readiness that comes from the gospel of peace.

EPHESIANS 6:13-15

Again, the descriptions of the individual pieces of the Roman armor would have had much more meaning to the original recipients of the letter than to modern Christians. We respond more readily to terms like bulletproof vest, riot squad helmet and shield, ammunition belt, and hiking boots. Yet, all of these terms are simply figures of speech to help us get a handle on the basic truth. Perhaps the best summary of the armor is in Romans 13:14, where Paul tells us: "Clothe yourselves with the Lord Jesus Christ."

The belt of truth, for example, is clearly Christ, the living Word of God and the expression of that truth in the Scriptures. Truth represents our commitment to follow the leadership of legitimate authority. A soldier who does not learn to follow orders is a detriment to an army and may be severely punished. There are too many soldiers in the Lord's army who may not say it in so many words but who live with the attitude, "No one is going to tell me what to do." The Scriptures have strong words for those who rebel against legitimate authority (see 1 Sm 15:23; Rom 13:1-5; 1 Pt 2:13-14). A good soldier learns to follow orders, for his own sake as well as the sake of his fellow soldiers. Christ is Lord, and his truth becomes our marching orders. Without truth there can be no effective battle plan for confronting this enemy.

Many other things hang on the belt of truth—our weapon, our ammunition clips, our canteen of refreshing water, our mess kit of food, and other items needed in the battle. The breastplate/flak jacket/bulletproof vest is defense against Satan as the "accuser" (Rv 12:10). If he accuses us of sin, and he is right, we simply agree with the Lord about it and receive his forgiveness (see 1 Jn 1:9). If the accusation is not true, we tell him to go to the cross and make his claim there; then we go on living, with the assurance that "there is now no con-demnation for those who are *in Christ Jesus*" (Rom 8:1, emphasis added). Being clothed with Christ is the secret to victory in this area.

Helmets we understand a bit better. We wear them for bik-ing, skating, hockey, and football, and for hard-hat construction jobs, as well as for military and police action. We know how crit-ical it is to protect the head and the brain. Going back to the figure of the brain as computer, if the computer crashes, then nothing else will matter very much. Yet it is not just the brain that matters; it is what goes into the brain. It is how that amaz-ing computer in our head is programmed. If we have learned to take every thought captive and make it obedient to Christ (see 2 Cor 10:5), we are safe from the attacks of the enemy on this vital part of our lives.

Mobility is also a key element in military strategy, so soldiers need good shoes. Paul refers to this part of our outfit as the "readiness that comes from the gospel of peace." There are many things that can be said about this figure, but perhaps the most important is that we must be available to the Commander to be sent wherever and whenever he chooses to send us. Fear is not to control us, only the word of our Leader. We must not only be willing to go, we must be ready to go. We must have

been through basic training and must be ready for our marching orders.

This army is not made up of volunteers. God never asks for
volunteers for this war. We are all in it, whether we want to be
or not. He just looks for those who are ready to submit their
wills to his in every area of their lives, so that he can use them
to reclaim territory from the enemy. This is another way of saying that he is looking for those who make Christ Lord—those
who "put on" the Lord Jesus Christ.[3]

"But," you ask, "I thought this was the gospel of peace. How
does that fit with warfare?" Our spiritual warfare is against the
one who robs a person of peace, and the message we bring is
the message that brings peace to a troubled soul. The problem
is that the enemy does not surrender his territory without resistance; we thus have to be prepared to enforce the victory that
Christ won at the cross whenever we meet this foe. We need to
know his tactics and go into the battle dressed in the "whole
armor" and equipped with the confidence that we are "more
than conquerors through him who loved us" (Rom 8:37).

Our enemy's offensive tactics begin with trying to gain a
foothold in our lives. Paul speaks of this in writing to the
Ephesians when he says, "In your anger do not sin. Do not let
the sun go down while you are still angry, and do not give the
devil a foothold" (Eph 4:26-27). Commenting on this, Clinton
Arnold says,

> It is likely that any sinful activity that the believer does not
> deal with by the power of the Spirit can be exploited by the
> devil and turned into a means of control over a believer's life.
> Therefore Christians need to resist.[4]

Footholds tend to be built on sins of the flesh, occult activity, unforgiveness, and lies.

The foothold that is not recognized and dealt with quickly becomes a stronghold, just as a beachhead in military strategy becomes a base for further invasion of enemy territory. A stronghold may be defined as a system of lies that gives the devil power in our lives. As Arnold says, the foothold of the first lie or the first sin becomes a means of control in a person's life. That does not mean that they become "demon possessed" and cannot live reasonably normal lives. It simply means that Satan has an established beachhead from which he can affect many other things in the person's life.

So, what do we do about strongholds?

The James 4:7 Strategy

A key passage in learning to deal with strongholds is James 4:7. The context of James 4 is the Christian's struggle with the world, the flesh, and the devil, and in this verse James says, "Submit yourselves ... to God. Resist the devil, and he will flee from you." The two key elements in dealing with spiritual strongholds are thus submission and resistance—submission to God and resistance of the devil.

What is involved in these two steps? The primary steps in submitting to God include: (1) confession of any sin or occult activity in our lives, 2) renouncing the sin and occult activity, (3) receiving forgiveness for those sins, (4) forgiving those who have wronged us, (5) renouncing the lies we have believed and affirming the truth, and (6) committing ourselves to God's truth as the basis for our lives.[5]

Confession is simply agreeing with God about anything that he calls sin. It means saying, "Yes, God, that was sin." Our view of sin is dependent on our view of God. If we have a low and defective view of God, we will have a low and defective view of sin. This takes us right back to where we began this discussion of spiritual warfare—Satan's attempts to corrupt our view of God.

Having confessed our sin, there are two further things we need to do in relation to it. First we need to renounce the sin. Renouncing means that we recognize why the sin is really sinful and condemned by a holy God, and we resolve to turn from it once and for all. Paul wrote to Titus, "For the grace of God has appeared bringing salvation to all, training us *to renounce* impiety and worldly passions, and in the present age to live lives that are self-controlled, upright, and godly (Ti 2:11-12, NRSV, emphasis added; see 2 Cor 4:1-2). Many years before, Solomon gave us the proverb that says, "He who conceals his sins does not prosper, but whoever confesses and *renounces* them finds mercy" (Prv 28:13, emphasis added). We too easily fall into the sin-confess-sin-confess cycle. When we sin, we should confess, renounce, and then resist.

Yet we also need to receive forgiveness. We need to believe that 1 John 1:9 is really true: "If we confess our sins, he is faithful and just and will forgive us our sins and purify us from all unrighteousness." There is a sense in which we do not even need to ask for forgiveness. We rather say, "Yes, God, that was sin. Thank you that Christ bore the penalty for the sin at the cross. I receive by faith what he did for me."

The second stage of the James 4:7 strategy is to resist the devil. How do we do that? Some teach or at least imply that submitting to God is the only kind of resisting we need to do.

This is not the picture we are given in the Old Testament. Israel had to go out and engage the enemy, even though the outcome was always determined by what God did, not what they did. I'm sure they would have been glad if all they had had to do was sit in their camp while God did all the fighting. That was seldom the way it worked for Israel, however, and the message of the New Testament is that the spiritual battle for us is not much different.

It is true that sometimes God seems to do all the fighting for us. Those are wonderful times, but the history of the church would indicate that God usually allows us to be actively engaged in this warfare. If God did all the fighting for us, we wouldn't need the armor and the weapons we are commanded to put on and use.

Authorized and Equipped for Battle

We need to remember that we resist from our position "in Christ." There are no tactics that will rout the enemy when employed by a person operating "in the flesh." We have already discussed this in chapter four. When we are in an up-to-date relationship with the Lord, we can be assured that we operate with divine authority behind us, and we are armed with the weapons and ammunition we need to press the battle with confidence.

The first of the weapons is the Word of God. This is the truth that nullifies the effect of Satan's primary tactic of deception. It is the light that dispels the darkness created by the one who "has blinded the minds of unbelievers, so that they cannot see the light of the gospel of the glory of Christ" (2 Cor 4:4). It is the

Word that is the "sword of the Spirit" (Eph 6:17). It is especially the Word as appropriated by us and spoken with trust and confidence. John tells us in Revelation 12 that the believers under attack by Satan overcame him "by the word of their testimony" (Rv 12:11). The Scriptures are not magical incantations to be used by just anyone, but when they are used as the testimony of one who is "in Christ" and who has proved the truthfulness of the Scriptures, they become the weapon that causes the enemy to flee.

Closely related to this is praise from the mouth of the child of God. Praise is a form of testimony. It is affirming the truth about God and about the victory of Christ. It is claiming victory before the victory is seen or experienced. Satan hates praise. God is "enthroned" on the praises of his people (see Ps 22:3, NASB). Praise invites the presence of God, and Satan wants to avoid that at all costs. The psalmist likens praise to a horn—a horn that summons the heavenly army to battle under the command of the Lord of Hosts (see Ps 148:14). In another place the psalmist says, "Before the 'gods' I will sing your praise" (Ps 138:1). The image is of looking our enemy in the eye and routing him by singing praise.

Prayer is another powerful weapon against this enemy. In Ephesians 6, Paul tells us to put on the armor, take up the sword, and then pray. You would expect him to say, "Now fight." The clear implication is that Paul sees prayer not as just a weapon, but as a part of the battle itself. Prayer is often where the "struggle" against the "the powers of this dark world and against supernatural forces of evil in the heavenly realms" is really fought. This is what leads S.D. Gordon to say, "Prayer is striking the winning blow at the concealed enemy. Service is gathering up the results of that blow among the [people] we see and touch."[6] This is why prayer is often difficult. Satan knows that if he can keep us from prayer, he can keep us from "striking the winning blow" in our battle against him. People often complain that when they try to pray, their minds wander, they get sleepy, or they think of a dozen other things to do. My response is, "Welcome to the war!" When you get into the thick of things, where the decisive battle is being fought, you have to expect the action to pick up.

Another factor in resisting the devil is the blood of Christ. Revelation 12:11 says of those whom the dragon, the devil, was attacking, "They overcame him by the blood of the Lamb and by the word of their testimony." We need to be careful about using the word *blood* or the expression *under the blood* as having power in and of themselves. As we have said, God does not use magical words or formulas. Yet the Scriptures say that by the blood we are redeemed (see Eph 1:7), justified (see Rom 5:9), cleansed (see 1 Jn 1:7), and made holy (see Heb 13:12), and by the blood we have confidence to enter the Most Holy Place (see Heb 10:19-22). If by faith we have appropriated these blessings, we are in a position to resist Satan's accusations and attacks. More than that, however, we are in a place where we can be a part of building Christ's church around the world—a church against which Christ promised that the gates of hell could not prevail (see Mt 16:18, KJV).

There are other weapons that could be identified,[7] but one stands out as essential for successful warfare—the name of Jesus. Again, the Bible makes it clear that we cannot use this name as a power word. In order to do anything "in the name" of another person, you first have to have an active relationship with that person and be commissioned by that person to act on his or her behalf. I cannot go around doing things "in the name of the president of the United States," for example, because I have not been commissioned by him to act in his stead. I could say the words, but no one would need to pay any attention to them. The same is true in seeking to act "in the name of Jesus" when resisting the demons. They don't have to pay any attention to the words, either. The seven sons of Sceva discovered this in a painful way (see Acts 19:13-16).

Yet we have been commissioned by our Lord Jesus Christ to go into the world and to make disciples of all nations, and with that commission comes the authority needed to carry it out. That doesn't mean that we can go anywhere we decide to go and assume the authority to act in his name, but when we go where he sends us, we can be assured that we have the authority we need to resist the devil. This begins in our personal lives and in our homes. Christian parents have the authority to cleanse and protect their home and family.[8] Christians also have the authority to invade territory long held by Satan and to build the church. We don't cast demons out of the places we go. If we could do that, planting churches would be easy. Through prayer, however, the enemy's power can be bound, and we can minister victoriously in spite of the worst the enemy can do.

Back to the Basics

Soldiers who have been in active combat often need to go back to boot camp to review the basics. Many Christian soldiers also need to go back to the basics. They have heard the teaching at some time in their growing-up years, but they have not been putting it into practice. They need a refresher. In this war, there is really no such thing as safe rear-echelon activity. Our spiritual enemy does not recognize spatial distance as we mortals do. This is why we need to be spiritually fit for battle at all times. We cannot afford to think that we are safe as long as we ignore the devil. Sooner or later he will take advantage of any area of weakness we allow to persist in our lives. He still comes to steal, kill, and destroy (see Jn 10:10). But with the proper uniform and with reasonable skill in using the weapons, we can be more than conquerors.

Here is how a pastor's wife described her experience of victory in a letter to me (Neil):

> How can I say thanks? The Lord allowed me to spend time with you just when I was concluding that there was no hope for me to ever break free from the downward spiral of continual defeat, depression, and guilt.
>
> Having literally grown up in church and being a pastor's wife for 25 years, everyone thought I was as put together on the inside as I was on the outside. On the contrary, I knew that there was no infrastructure on the inside and often wondered when the weight of trying to hold myself together would cause my life to fall apart and come crumbling down. It seemed as if sheer determination was the only thing that kept me going.
>
> When I left your office last Thursday it was a beautiful crystal clear day with the snow visible on the mountains, and it felt like a film had been lifted from over my eyes. The tape player was playing … "It Is Well With My Soul." The words of the song fairly exploded in my mind with the realization that it was well in my soul for the first time in years.
>
> The next day in the office … I heard, "Boy, something must have happened to you yesterday."

I have heard the same songs and read the same Bible verses as before, but it is as if I'm really hearing for the first time. There is underlying joy and peace in the midst of the same circumstances that used to bring defeat and discouragement....

Already the deceiver has tried to plant thoughts in my mind and tell me that this won't last; it is just another gimmick that won't work. The difference is that now I know those are lies from Satan and not the truth. What a difference freedom in Christ makes!

■ ■

NINE

Fit for Battle

One of the big challenges for military commanders is to keep their troops battle-ready when they are not involved in real combat. When soldiers are in an active battle situation they know how important mental and physical conditioning is, but when they are in a safe place in a time of peace it is all too easy to become focused on things that have little to do with being a soldier. The difference between military warfare and spiritual warfare is that we are always in the battle, whether we realize it or not. The difference is that in spiritual warfare the enemy cannot be seen. Our struggle is not against people with flesh and bones but against spirits from the realm of Satan. People may well become involved in the struggle as the instruments Satan uses against us, but the real battle is spiritual.

This means that we always need to be battle-ready. There is no such thing as a safe place, if by that we mean a place where the enemy is not a present threat. The only sanctuary we have is our position "in Christ." We are not helpless victims in this war, but we are told to be always on guard, because we never know when or where the enemy will launch one of his deceptive attacks.

This is a beginner's guide to spiritual warfare. That is why we have confined our discussion to being fit for battle through spiritual preparedness and have not gone into some of the more advanced levels of such warfare. Too often well-meaning believers fall into one of two traps. They either try to stay out of the war by ignoring it, or they try to get involved at a level for which they are not prepared. For both, the place to begin is to recognize the real nature of the battle and then to get the basic training needed to be ready when the Commander calls us to more direct involvement.

Warfare can be looked at from two different perspectives—offensive and defensive. The Scriptures speak of both in this spiritual battle. We are told, on the one hand, to be prepared to defend ourselves against the attacks of the enemy (see Eph 6:10-18; 1 Pt 5:8-9), but we are also told to pray, "Your kingdom come" (Mt 6:10). If God's kingdom is to come, Satan's kingdom (see Mt 12:26; Col 1:13; Rv 9:11; 16:10) must come down. This involves spiritual warfare. We are also commanded to be a part of that invasion of Satan's kingdom. Jesus sends his disciples "into all the world" (Mk 16:15)—the world over which Satan rules—and he sends them in order to bring people "from darkness to light, and from the power of Satan to God" (Acts 26:18). Even today this Great Commission continues to tell us to go and make disciples (see Mt 28:18-20), and we can do that by crossing the ocean or just crossing the street. It can be accomplished through our witness at work or at school. It can be accomplished through intercession. It can be accomplished through stewardship of our resources. In any case, you know Satan does not want this to happen, and he will do everything he can to prevent our fruitful participation in such activity.

Thus, the battle is not "way over there somewhere"; it is all around us. We do not first enter the battle when we become involved in some active "ministry." The battle may intensify when we do, but Satan knows that he can prevent ministry involvement if he can keep us from basic training. God sends as laborers only those who have been through boot camp—those who are battle-ready. If we are not prepared, we will probably not want to go; and if we go out of a sense of obligation rather than through the clear working of the Spirit of God within us, we will probably become part of the problem rather than part of the answer. Incompatibility among missionaries is one of the chief reasons for the high rate of fallout among first-term missionaries. When this happens, we have to recognize that there is a spirit at work other than the Spirit of Christ. Two Spirit-led believers are not going to find themselves incompatible. Yes, there may be personality differences, but this is part of God's plan. We need each other. When such things cause us to be ineffective in our ministries, it can only mean that someone's personality is not under the Spirit's control or that someone is not doing things God's way. The result is that Satan is the one who smiles with approval.

We saw an example of this when we were asked to minister to a team of believers involved in potentially productive ministry. The problem was that there was a great deal of discouragement among the team and some had recently left the ministry. One was quoted as saying, "Why do we have to have an outsider come in to talk to us? We can't even talk to each other civilly!" It did not take long to discover that there were many things in that ministry that had either been overlooked or had never been looked at through God's eyes. Many learned for the first time how to get their sense of identity from their relationship to an unconditionally loving God rather than from a dysfunctional family or a dysfunctional ministry team. One leader admitted that he was very defensive when he felt threatened in relations with colleagues, rather than being an example of trust and resting in the Lord. We also readily identified a number of occult practices in connection with the place of ministry.

As the truth began to replace the deceptions of the enemy, and as the truth was acted on by individuals, the result was a report that "we saw interpersonal conflicts and team internal conflicts begin to be resolved." As they learned to practice forgiveness and reconciliation based on their renewed relationships with the Lord, the ministry team reported that this was becoming evident even in the way they conducted business meetings and carried on day-to-day operations.

Satan's plan for the church is to divide, discourage, and destroy. History testifies to the fact that he has all too often been very successful with that strategy. The reason for this has to be that, on the one hand, we have been ignorant of his tactics (see 2 Cor 2:11) and, on the other hand, we have not been fit for battle. Satan loves to be ignored. That allows him to go about his deceptive work of keeping the church from marching "like a mighty army," as it is evident God intended it to do.

Consider the following testimony from a pastor who readily offered to let us share this experience to encourage others:

> In 1993 I ... began applying your principles to my problems. I realized that some of my problems could be spiritual attacks, and I learned how to take a stand....
>
> I was a deacon and preacher in a small Baptist church. My pastor was suffering from depression and other problems,... and in 1994 he committed suicide. This literally brought our church to its knees....
>
> The church elected me as their Interim Pastor. While in a

local bookstore I saw a book of yours [Neil's] on *Setting Your Church Free*. I purchased and read it. I felt with all the spiritual oppression in our church this was the answer. Only one problem—to get the rest of the church to believe.... The previous pastor would never read or listen to your message.

Slowly, very slowly, the people accepted my messages, and [Mike Quarles][1] led the leaders of our church through the "Setting Your Church Free." The leaders loved it.... Six weeks later, I was able to take all the people through the "Seven Steps to Freedom." I really don't understand it, but we were set free from the spiritual bondage of multiple problems. I can't put it in a letter or I would write a book.

During all of this one of my middle-aged members, who was an evangelist, was set free, learned who he is in Christ, and is back in the ministry.... I saw the twin daughters of the deceased pastor set free and able to forgive their father.... At one point one of the twins was contemplating suicide.

This is a new church; God is free to work here!

We are in a battle, whether we want to be or not. The only question is whether we will fight well, poorly, or not at all. Our Commander has provided the best of armor and weapons, yet they will bring victory only when we use them. If you have not been through spiritual boot camp, the reading list at the end of this book is a good place to begin, and *The Steps to Freedom in Christ* (a small booklet) will guide you in applying the truth to key areas of your life. Don't give the enemy the satisfaction of neutralizing you in this battle.

NOTES

INTRODUCTION

1. I first reported these findings in *Rivers of Revival* (Ventura, Calif.: Regal, 1997), which I co-authored with Dr. Elmer Towns.

2. Joe Aldrich, *Prayer Summits* (Portland, Ore.: Multnomah, 1992).

ONE
A Reluctant Warrior?

1. By God's providence, the position of chaplain's assistant came open shortly before we left for overseas duty in the combat zone, and while I spent many months where the fighting was taking place, I was able to serve in an area of positive ministry rather than as a fighter.

2. Quoted by Leon Morris in the Tyndale New Testament Commentary on *The First Epistle of Paul to the Corinthians* (Grand Rapids, Mich.: Eerdmans, 1958), 85.

3. See Neil Anderson and Rich Miller, *Freedom From Fear* (Eugene, Ore.: Harvest House, 1999), for a full discussion of fear.

TWO
Is This Spiritual Warfare or Plain Old Trouble?

1. See Neil Anderson, *Victory over the Darkness* (Ventura, Calif.: Regal, 1990) for a fuller discussion of what happened in the Fall.

2. The NIV translates the Greek word *sarx* as "sinful nature." This raises too many theological questions to be a desirable translation. I much prefer to stay with the literal rendering as "flesh."

3. See Neil Anderson and Robert Saucy, *The Common Made Holy* (Eugene, Ore.: Harvest House, 1997), 312–22, for a full discussion of the flesh.

4. Arndt and Gingrich, *A Greek-English Lexicon of the New Testament* (Chicago: Univ. of Chicago Press, 1957), 750–52.

5. I learned this definition very early in my study of anthropology, but unfortunately I do not have the original source. I think it was from the writings of Eugene Nida.

6. See Clinton Arnold, *Three Crucial Questions About Spiritual Warfare* (Grand Rapids, Mich.: Baker, 1997), 32–37, for a helpful discussion of this balance.

7. Neil Anderson, *Living Free in Christ* (Ventura, Calif.: Regal, 1993).

THREE
Toward a Biblical Worldview

1. James Sire, *The Universe Next Door* (Downers Grove, Ill.: InterVarsity, 1976), 17.

2. For a discussion of worldview as filters, see Charles Kraft, *Christianity with Power* (Ann Arbor, Mich.: Servant, 1989), 18–19.

3. Joel Belz, "Believing Everything," *World*, April 25, 1998, 5.

4. For a scholarly treatment of the worldview of Bible times see Clinton Arnold's two books *Powers of Darkness* (Downers Grove, Ill.: InterVarsity, 1992) and *Ephesians: Power and Magic* (Grand Rapids, Mich.: Baker, 1992).

5. John Warwick Montgomery, *Principalities and Powers, Revised and Enlarged Edition* (Minneapolis: Dimension, 1975), 165–66.

6. For a further discussion of this issue, see Zeb Long and Douglas McMurry, *The Collapse of the Brass Heaven* (Grand Rapids, Mich.: Chosen, 1994) and Gregory Boyd, *God at War* (Downers Grove, Ill.: InterVarsity, 1997). The latter book is especially good in its scholarly presentation of the "warfare worldview" of the Bible.

7. The category of "things" could be broken down into animal, vegetable, and mineral, but that is not relevant to our present discussion. It would be relevant if we were looking more comprehensively at worldview as found in various human societies.

FOUR
More Than Technique

1. See Neil Anderson, *The Bondage Breaker* (Eugene, Ore.: Harvest House, 1990), for a guide to taking an in-depth look at your spiritual life.

2. Neil Anderson and Pete and Sue Vander Hook, *Spiritual Protection for Your Children* (Ventura, Calif.: Regal, 1996).

3. See Neil Anderson and Steve Russo, *The Seduction of Our Children* (Eugene, Ore.: Harvest House, 1991), 23.

FIVE
Who Am I, Really?

1. We can also overemphasize the work of the Holy Spirit and fail to balance that with an emphasis on truth that is to be believed and commands that are to be obeyed.

SIX

Which God Do I Serve?

1. Daniel B. Wallace, "Who's Afraid of the Holy Spirit?" *Christianity Today,* September 12, 1994, 35–38.
2. Wallace, 37.

SEVEN

Keep Looking Down

1. See Anderson, *Victory over the Darkness* and Anderson and Saucy, *The Common Made Holy,* for a full discussion of this truth.
2. Anderson, *Victory over the Darkness,* 43.
3. For a very helpful treatment of this concept, see Jeff VanVonderen, *Tired of Trying to Measure Up* (Minneapolis: Bethany House, 1989).
4. Dr. and Mrs. Howard Taylor, *Hudson Taylor and the China Inland Mission: The Growth of a Work of God* (London: Morgan and Scott, 1918), 175.
5. Jean S. Pigott, "Jesus, I Am Resting, Resting," *Hymns* (Chicago: InterVarsity, 1952), 139.
6. Anderson, *The Bondage Breaker,* 70.

EIGHT

Boot Camp for Reluctant Warriors

1. See C.S. Lewis, *The Screwtape Letters* (New York: Macmillan, 1961), for an insightful look at the coaching demons receive.
2. See Clinton Arnold, *Ephesians: Power and Magic,* for a scholarly treatment of this subject.
3. For a fuller treatment of the armor, see D. Martyn Lloyd-Jones, *The Christian Soldier* (Grand Rapids, Mich.: Baker, 1977), and Mark Bubeck, *Overcoming the Adversary* (Chicago: Moody, 1984).
4. Arnold, *Powers of Darkness,* 128.
5. See "The Steps to Freedom in Christ" in Anderson, *The Bondage Breaker,* pages 185–204, for guidance in doing this.
6. S.D. Gordon, *Quiet Talks on Prayer* (Grand Rapids, Mich.: Baker, 1980), 19.
7. See K. Neill Foster, *Warfare Weapons* (Camp Hill, Penn.: Christian Publications, 1995).
8. See Anderson and Vander Hook, *Spiritual Protection for Your Children;* Anderson and Russo, *The Seduction of Our Children;* Mark Bubeck, *Raising Lambs Among Wolves,* (Chicago: Moody, 1997); and Chuck Pierce and Rebecca Sytsema, *Ridding Your Home of Spiritual Darkness* (Colorado Springs, Colo.: Wagner Institute, 1999).

NINE

Fit for Battle

1. Fit for Battle Freedom in Christ staff, co-author with Neil of *Freedom from Addiction* (Ventura, Calif.: Regal, 1996).

Anderson, Neil. *The Bondage Breaker.* Eugene, Ore: Harvest House, 1990.

    Daily in Christ. Eugene, Ore.: Harvest House, 1993.

    Helping Others Find Freedom in Christ. Ventura, Calif.: Regal, 1995.

    Living Free in Christ. Ventura, Calif.: Regal, 1993.

    Released from Bondage. Nashville, Tenn.: Nelson, 1993.

    The Steps to Freedom in Christ. Ventura, Calif.: Gospel Light, 1996.

    Victory over the Darkness. Ventura, Calif.: Regal, 1990.

    Walking in the Light. Nashville, Tenn.: Nelson, 1993.

Anderson, Neil, and Rich Miller, *Freedom From Fear* (Eugene, Ore.: Harvest House, 1999).

Anderson, Neil, and Charles Mylander. *Setting Your Church Free.* Ventura, Calif.: Regal, 1994.

Anderson, Neil, and Steve Russo. *The Seduction of Our Children.* Eugene, Ore.: Harvest House, 1991.

Anderson, Neil, and Robert Saucy. *The Common Made Holy.* Eugene, Ore.: Harvest House, 1997.

Anderson, Neil, and Pete and Sue Vander Hook. *Spiritual Protection for Your Children.* Ventura, Calif.: Regal, 1996.

Arnold, Clinton. *Ephesians: Power and Magic.* Cambridge: Cambridge Univ. Press, 1989, and Grand Rapids, Mich.: Baker, 1992.

    Powers of Darkness: Principalities and Powers in Paul's Letters. Downers Grove, Ill.: InterVarsity, 1992.

    Three Crucial Questions About Spiritual Warfare. Grand Rapids, Mich.: Baker, 1997.

Beeson, Ray, and Kathi Mills. *Spiritual Warfare and Your Children*. Nashville, Tenn.: Nelson, 1993.

Bubeck, Mark I. *The Adversary*. Chicago: Moody, 1974.

Overcoming the Adversary. Chicago: Moody, 1984.

Raising Lambs Among Wolves. Chicago: Moody, 1997.

Foster, K. Neill. *Binding and Loosing: Exercising Authority Over the Dark Powers*. Camp Hill, Penn.: Christian Publications, 1998.

Gordon, S.D. *Quiet Talks on Prayer*. Grand Rapids, Mich.: Baker, 1980.

Graham, Billy. *Angels: God's Secret Agents*. Garden City, N.Y.: Doubleday, 1975.

Gurnall, William. *The Christian in Complete Armor: A Modernized Abridgement*. 3 vols. Carlisle, Penn.: Banner of Truth, 1986 (orig. published in 1655).

Larson, Bob. *Straight Answers on the New Age*. Nashville, Tenn.: Nelson, 1989.

Lewis, C.S. *The Screwtape Letters*. New York: Macmillan, 1961.

Logan, Jim. *Reclaiming Surrendered Ground*. Chicago: Moody, 1995.

Long, Zeb, and Douglas McMurry. *The Collapse of the Brass Heaven: Rebuilding Our Worldview to Embrace the Power of God*. Grand Rapids, Mich.: Chosen, 1994.

Michaelson, Johanna. *The Beautiful Side of Evil*. Eugene, Ore.: Harvest House, 1982.

Like Lambs to the Slaughter: Your Child and the Occult. Eugene, Ore.: Harvest House, 1988.

Moreau, A. Scott. *The Essentials of Spiritual Warfare*. Wheaton, Ill.: Shaw, 1997

Murphy, Ed. *The Handbook for Spiritual Warfare*. Nashville, Tenn.: Nelson, 1992.

Phillips, Phil. *Turmoil in the Toybox*. Lancaster, Penn.: Starburst, 1986.

Porter, David. *Children at Risk: The Growing Threat of Bizarre Toys, Fantasy Games, TV, Movies, and Illegal Drugs*. Wheaton, Ill.: Crossway, 1987.

Robie, Joan Hake. *Turmoil in the Toybox II*. Lancaster, Penn.: Starburst, 1986.

Sanders, J. Oswald. *Satan Is No Myth*. Chicago: Moody, 1975.

Sherrer, Quin, and Ruthanne Garlock. *The Spiritual Warrior's Prayer Guide*. Ann Arbor, Mich.: Servant, 1992.

Wagner, C. Peter. *Praying With Power*. Ventura, Calif.: Regal, 1997.

Warner, Timothy. *Spiritual Warfare: Victory over the Powers of This Dark World*. Wheaton: Crossway, 1991.

Weldon, John, and James Bjornstad. *Playing With Fire: Fantasy Games*. Chicago: Moody, 1984.

White, Thomas B. *The Believer's Guide to Spiritual Warfare*. Ann Arbor, Mich.: Servant, 1990.

Breaking Strongholds. Ann Arbor, Mich.: Servant, 1993.

Other Books in the *Beginner's Guide* series include:

The Beginner's Guide to the Gift of Prophecy
by Jack Deere

The Beginner's Guide to Intercession
by Dutch Sheets

The Beginner's Guide to Fasting
by Elmer Towns

The Beginner's Guide to Spiritual Gifts
by Sam Storms

The Beginner's Guide to Receiving the Holy Spirit
by Quin Sherrer and Ruthanne Garlock

Ask for them at your nearest Christian bookstore.

Get the Whole Series

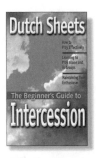

The Beginner's Guide to Intercession
Dutch Sheets
ISBN 08307.33914

The Beginner's Guide to the Gift of Prophecy
Jack Deere
ISBN 08307.33892

The Beginner's Guide to Fasting
Elmer Towns
ISBN 08307.33884

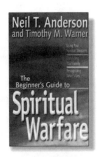

The Beginner's Guide to Spiritual Warfare
Neil T. Anderson and Timothy M. Warner
ISBN 08307.33876

The Beginner's Guide to Praise and Worship
Gary Kinnaman
ISBN 08307.33949

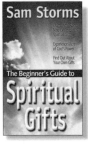

The Beginner's Guide to Spiritual Gifts
Sam Storms
ISBN 08307.33922

The Beginner's Guide to Receiving the Holy Spirit
Quin Sherrer and Ruthanne Garlock
ISBN 08307.33930

The Beginner's Guide to Hearing God
Jim Goll
ISBN 08307.34503

Pick Up a Copy at Your Favorite Christian Bookstore!

Visit **www.regalbooks.com** to join Regal's **FREE** e-newsletter. You'll get useful **excerpts from our newest releases** and **special access to online chats with your favorite authors.** Sign up today!

God's Word for Your World™
www.regalbooks.com